Gooseberry Patch

Christmas

with Family & Friends

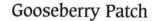

Gooseberry Patch

An imprint of Globe Pequot
246 Goose Lane
Guilford, CT 06437

www.gooseberrypatch.com
1·800·854·6673

Copyright 2022, Gooseberry Patch 978-1-62093-475-3

Do you have a tried & true recipe...

tip, craft or memory that you'd like to see featured in a **Gooseberry Patch** cookbook? Visit our website at **www.gooseberrypatch.com** and follow the easy steps to submit your favorite family recipe. Or send them to us at:

Gooseberry Patch
PO Box 812
Columbus, OH 43216-0812

Don't forget to include the number of servings your recipe makes, plus your name, address, phone number and email address. If we select your recipe, your name will appear right along with it...and you'll receive a **FREE** copy of the book!

Contents

Dedication

Dedicated to those who love hand-knit stockings, woolly mittens and gifts from the heart.

Appreciation

To our family & friends... thank you for making our holidays warm & cozy.

TINSEL
GARLAND

ORNAMENT

Homemade *Memories*

Our Christmas Miracle

Hope Davenport
Portland, TX

My husband, our three children and I will never forget the Christmas of 2004. We live in South Texas, and the children and I had never seen snow. This particular Christmas Eve, our families were gathered at my parents' home when a report of snow flurries was heard on the news. We went outside and were very excited...especially since it hadn't snowed here in 75 years. The kids and I forgot all about the presents and spent most of the night outside taking pictures and video of the snow! We had so much fun, but assumed that the little specks falling from the sky were as much as we could expect in South Texas. We never dreamed we would awake to a snow-covered town on Christmas morning. It must have snowed all night because when we woke up the town was covered with 3 to 4 inches of snow. It was so beautiful and I finally understood what people mean when they say how quiet it is after a snowfall. Now, around here, we can usually wear shorts on Christmas day, so this was quite a change. We had no mittens and were not at all prepared for this surprise! We had to use socks and oven mitts to keep our hands warm during snowball fights and while making snow angels and snowmen. The snow slowly melted that day, but not before we had hours of fun and made many wonderful memories. To have snow in South Texas was an amazing thing to see, but for it to actually happen on Christmas Eve and wake up to a beautiful white Christmas, it felt like a miracle.

What Did Santa Forget?

Kate Finch
Torrington, CT

After all the Christmas presents have been opened, dinner has been enjoyed and relatives have started their travels home, just as we were ready for bed, something special would happen. My mother would always come in from outside saying she found a snow-covered bag at the bottom of the chimney that Santa had "forgotten." It was so exciting as we all would have one more really special present to open before bedtime...a capper on an already special day.

Hunting for the Christmas Tree

Melissa Fialer
Palo Alto, CA

As a little girl growing up in California, I didn't enjoy the very cold days in the winter that led up to Christmas. However, my parents would create "magical moments" for my sister and me during those days. About three weeks before Christmas, my whole family would pile into our station wagon and drive up a long winding road into the mountains to a Christmas tree ranch. My dad would be delegated to carry the saw and do the cutting, while my mom and sister and I went searching for just the right tree. It was like a game of Marco Polo, hearing each others' voices around the tree farm trying to find just the right one, then came the big moment..."I found it!" It would be the perfect tree...bushy and not too tall with a wonderful fragrance. Absolutely perfect! After my dad would cut it down, it was roped to the top of our car, then we spent the drive down the hill making sure the tree wasn't going to slide off. Once we were home, the tree was placed in our family room...that was when the popcorn started popping, the carols started playing and the tree came to life. My sister and I would string popcorn and cranberries on thread, while my mom made fudge, date petit-fours and all manner of goodies that made the house smell like heaven to me. The day stood on its own in my memories and truly has always defined what preparing for Christmas is all about..family and traditions.

A Magical Christmas Tree Stand

Maryann Brett
Johnstown, PA

When I was a small child in the early 1960s, the one thing I can remember the most about every Christmas was our Christmas tree. Well, not exactly the tree, but rather the stand that the tree was placed in. The stand was very special, and to us kids, it was somewhat magical, for we had a tree stand like no other I had ever seen. Attached to the stand was a small black box with three switches on it. One switch would make the stand revolve in circles, one switch would turn on all the Christmas lights and the last switch would play Christmas music. I can still hear the music in my head! It was always fun to be the first one up on Christmas morning to "turn on the tree." That tree stand always had a live Christmas tree in it and you could fill the bottom with water to keep it fresh. It was decorated with lights that looked like colored popcorn balls, glass balls and other decorations we had made by hand. That tree stand was bought in the early 1950s before I was born and lasted well into the 1990s. As we children grew up, married, and started our own families, we would take turns sharing the tree stand for our own family to enjoy. When the time came that the tree stand could finally turn no more, my sister made a tape of the Christmas music it played so we could continue to enjoy it. Thinking back, ours was the only house I ever knew of with a special Christmas tree stand like that one, and it will always bring back special memories of my childhood!

JINGLE BELLS...

MUSICAL TREE STAND

Christmas Eve Santa Radar

Beth Williamson
Oak Vale, MS

As my children were growing up, we would always gather together on Christmas Eve and exchange Christmas presents. After opening our gifts, we watched the evening news. As soon as the kids saw Santa on the radar, they were ready to jump into bed hoping that his next stop would be our house...this was such an exciting time! Even as my children have grown, this tradition has never stopped...it has now become a tradition with their friends as well. On Christmas Eve we still had our family time of opening gifts, then, just before the ten o'clock news, I hear cars driving up as some of their friends came to see where Santa was on the radar. My children are now 22, 26 and 29 and it's just as exciting now to see who will drive up at ten o'clock to watch with us. Afterward, everyone rushes home, to get into bed so that Santa will come to their house!

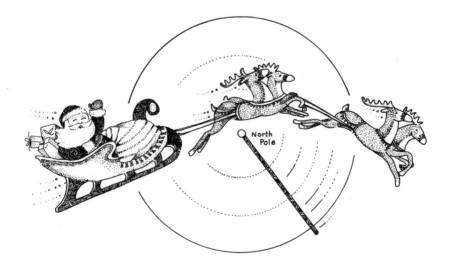

Christmas Memories

Linda Taylor
Nebo, KY

My Christmas memories continue year after year. I am now 54 years old and have never missed a Christmas celebration with our large family. We meet at my mother's home...cousins, children and grandchildren are always there. Our traditions include reading the Christmas story from the Bible, and then I'm always called upon to lead everyone in a hilarious round of singing "The Twelve Days of Christmas." Imagine approximately forty to fifty people of all ages singing the many verses! It is always a wonderful time and a night filled with memories that we all keep with us throughout the year. I hope my children and grandchildren will always remember and carry on these strong traditions.

Advent Calendar Memory

Jessica Daul
Oconto Falls, WI

One of my fondest memories is from when I was a little girl. My mother had an Advent calendar that she brought out the day after Thanksgiving as we started decorating for Christmas. My brother and I would admire it and couldn't wait for December 1st to come around! The calendar was made of cardboard with lots of bright colors. It was shaped like a house and each day of December, another decoration was added to complete the holiday scene. Each piece would have the day of the month on it, and when completed it would make a beautiful picture of a family surrounding a Christmas tree in their home. Every morning my brother and I would race down the stairs to see who would be able to attach the next piece first. Day after day this continued until Christmas Eve. This day had the best piece of all...the Christmas tree! After many years of use, a new Advent calendar was bought to replace this one. Looking back, we didn't realize at the time how much we would all remember and cherish the original one.

Angel Tree

Pamela Ferrand
Baton Rouge, LA

Every mid-November my children choose a name from their school's Angel Tree. They earn extra money to buy their Angel gifts by doing extra chores around our home and our neighborhood. This year, my two were really old enough to understand that some families have a harder time during the holiday season. As we were preparing to do our holiday shopping, my son said, "Mom, please add half of my Christmas money to my Angel's gift, I already have way too many toys and things. Since this child only wants a pair of shoes from Santa, I want him to have a Christmas to remember. I have so many good memories of our Christmases, I want to have at least one he can remember too." Well, this touched my heart deeply, and we did give that child a special Christmas. And I think that we got a special present too...I realized that my children really do learn from the things I try to teach them, and this year, he learned what it's like to give rather than receive.

A Family Christmas

Laurie Loftis
Ashland, OH

When my sister and I were preschoolers, Mom and Dad bought us
bride dolls. They were porcelain dolls, each wearing a satin dress
topped with lace and tulle with seed pearls. Although we didn't have
a lot of money, these dolls were something that my dad wanted us
to have. Early in my life, I realized the magic of Christmas and the
importance of making it special. We moved into our house 28 years
ago and over that span of time, the size of the house has gone from
750 square feet to almost 2,500 square feet. My husband and I have
no children of our own, but we have 20 nieces and nephews. Mom
gave me the tree that had been part of our family Christmases since
I was 10 years old. I still have it along with 31 trees, 15 nativities
and three villages that I put up every year. Our nieces and nephews
know that every year there is going to be something different,
whether it is a tree, ornaments, or another village piece. My parents
and grandparents instilled the wonder of Christmas in my heart.
Now, I want to carry on that tradition and instill it in my family.

Hand Cookies

Deborah Barrs
Orlando, FL

When it's time for me to start baking holiday cookies, a memory of my four sons making their hand cookies comes to mind. What a wonderful memory and tradition that started with my first son over 30 years ago. I would lay out their little hands on the cookie dough and gently and carefully cut around them, then bake those sweet hand cookies with the rest of the holiday cookies. The boys would all line up, side-by-side in front of their cookie shaped from their own hand, each decorating theirs in their very own style. I really created this idea to keep them busy while I decorated the batch of cookies, but instead, what fun memories it has created for me. Their hands have grown from tiny to large, to where only two cutouts would fit on the cookie sheet at a time. One year someone suggested making foot cookies instead...how we laughed! Sometimes I wish I could take time back to where we all were together laughing and joking with each other. Who knows...I might even let them do their feet this time! Thanks to my sons for the wonderful memories. It must have meant something to them, also, because last year one of my sons called me and asked if I would make the hand cookies with my grandson. I love Christmas and I feel that it is a perfect time to bring out the old traditions and even create new ones. Now I get to share this tradition with my grandchildren and create all-new memories.

Gingerbread Birdhouse

Jaime Madden
Portsmouth, OH

Each year my children and I make gingerbread houses to display in our kitchen during the holidays. I always hated tossing them away after Christmas, so one year, on a cold January day, I decided we could easily recycle them into bird and squirrel feeders. It was so much fun and the kids made all the neighborhood wildlife very happy. My daughter said the best part of all the fun was that she made two gingerbread houses in one year.

It's so easy...remove any hard candies and candy canes from the gingerbread house. Generously spread peanut butter over the house as if you were icing the house to decorate it. Decorate the house with lots of wildlife-friendly food..a door made of crackers, corner posts of pretzel sticks, a roof covered in shredded wheat cereal, raisin and bird seed-covered walls. Your family will really enjoy seeing the birds and squirrels that come to visit, but place the house off the ground. The neighbor's dog ate our first gingerbread birdhouse, so now we place it in an area he can't reach!

Christmas All Year

Lauren Williams
Kewanee, MO

One year after Christmas I bought a small artificial tree for $3.00 at a drugstore. I stored it in a closet with the intention of setting it up in my daughter's bedroom. One day I found my daughter and son playing Christmas in their bedroom. They had cut out drawings for ornaments and were using newspaper to wrap old toys to give one another. Now, whenever they get bored, I suggest that they play Christmas using small toys for ornaments and a roll of Christmas paper. They play for hours and the Christmas cheer lasts all year long. I would have never thought that a Christmas tree would have been as much fun to them as any toy they received.

Baking with My Sister

Sandy Pilarski
Wildwood, MO

My sister, Linda, is 16 years older than me and I have never outgrown how much I look up to her and respect her. When Linda was in college, I was, of course, hanging out at our house with my parents and anxiously awaiting all of her visits home. Linda was taking classes to become a teacher and I was her unwitting guinea pig for the projects she had been assigned. I always felt special that she'd pull out items for me to color, cut or paste from the worn suitcase that also released her special perfume to waft through the air as the top flipped open. One holiday season I remember especially well; I must have been about four years old. Linda was planning to arrive home a few days before Christmas and since she was a college student, she didn't have much money for Christmas gifts. Her plan was to return home, purchase all the necessary ingredients and bake like crazy while leaving enough time to get the goodies wrapped for the holiday. I was so excited just for her to be home, but when she asked if I wanted to help her with her baking project, I was in pure heaven. She had a huge copper container that she planned to fill...then and only then would she consider herself done. We started early that day and were still going strong in the wee hours of the next morning...and she didn't tell me once that I needed to go to bed. I think I did end up turning in before she did, but I had made that decision myself. Rumor has it that she was pulling out the last cookie sheet as the sun came up. That baking marathon with my big sister remains one of my favorite Christmas memories. My treat, my gift, had been time with someone who remains a special person in my life!

Vickie

Breakfast & Brunch with Friends

Scrumptious French Toast

Jackie Bell
Saint Augustine, FL

My father was a chef, and as he cooked, he would always add a pinch of this and a little of that. When I brought this dish to our men's pancake breakfast at church, it was a big hit. It's so easy to make and quite a treat for breakfast.

1 loaf French bread, sliced
8 eggs, beaten
1 pt. half-and-half
1 c. milk
1 t. vanilla extract

1-1/4 t. cinnamon, divided
1 t. nutmeg, divided
1 c. butter
1 c. brown sugar, packed
2 T. light corn syrup

Place bread slices into a greased 13"x9" baking pan; overlap if necessary. Whisk together eggs, half-and-half, milk, vanilla, 1/2 teaspoon cinnamon and 1/4 teaspoon nutmeg. Using an electric mixer on medium speed, beat for one minute. Pour mixture over bread slices and between any overlapping slices. Cover with aluminum foil and refrigerate overnight. The next day, prepare topping by blending butter and brown sugar with a pastry blender until mixture resembles coarse crumbs. Stir in corn syrup and remaining cinnamon and nutmeg. Spread mixture evenly over bread. Bake, uncovered, at 350 degrees for 25 to 30 minutes, until bread puffs and becomes golden. Makes 14 to 16 servings.

Enjoy a cozy winter's morning...serve white hot chocolate sprinkled with a dusting of cocoa powder.

Butterscotch Banana Waffles

Charmie Fisher
Fontana, CA

This is a family favorite that combines the homemade goodness of Grandma's butterscotch banana bread with waffles. My kids and grandkids have been enjoying these waffles for many years. A handy tip to remember...wipe off any melted butterscotch from the waffle iron between batches.

2-1/4 c. all-purpose flour	1/4 c. brown sugar, packed
1/2 t. baking powder	3 eggs, separated
1/2 t. baking soda	2 c. buttermilk
1/2 t. salt	2 ripe bananas, mashed
1 t. cinnamon	1 c. butterscotch chips
1/2 t. nutmeg	Optional: maple syrup or butter

Sift together flour, baking powder, baking soda, salt, cinnamon, nutmeg and brown sugar in a large bowl. In a separate large bowl, beat egg yolks. Stir in buttermilk and mashed bananas; stir in dry ingredients until well blended; set aside. Using an electric mixer at high speed, beat egg whites until stiff peaks form. Fold into batter. Gently stir in butterscotch chips. Heat a waffle iron and spray with non-stick vegetable spray. Pour the recommended amount of batter onto the iron and cook according to manufacturer's instructions until golden. Serve with maple syrup or butter, if desired. Makes 6 to 8 servings.

Dress up a store-bought stocking in a flurry. Use a pencil to lightly draw a star on the front. With a needle and craft thread, sew buttons directly on the stocking over the star outline.

Friendship Quiche

Lori Comer
Kernersville, NC

This is a wonderful recipe given to me by a friend. The French fried onions really give it a fabulous flavor. I bake this quiche every Christmas and take it to our office...our maintenance man always seems to come by at just the right time for the last slice!

1 refrigerated pie crust	6 eggs, beaten
1-1/3 c. French fried onions, divided	1 c. half-and-half or milk
	1/2 c. bacon bits
1-1/2 c. shredded sharp Cheddar cheese	Optional: 1/2 green pepper, finely chopped

Unfold pie crust and place in a 9" pie plate. Sprinkle 3/4 cup onions evenly over bottom of crust; sprinkle with cheese. In a medium bowl, whisk together eggs, half-and-half or milk, bacon bits and green pepper, if using. Pour mixture over cheese. Bake at 350 degrees for 30 minutes, or until center tests done. Sprinkle remaining onions on top. Bake an additional 5 minutes, or until golden. Let stand 5 minutes before slicing. Makes 8 servings.

Pretty farmhouse containers help keep wrapping supplies close at hand. Try new spins on old favorites...clothespins are perfect for keeping gift tags together, while small enamel pails are ideal for corralling pens, glue, ribbon, rubber stamps and tape.

Heidi's Breakfast Pizza

Heidi Markhart
Saginaw, MI

I'm always looking for new recipes to try and creating recipes of my own. This recipe was a sure-fire hit with my family... it had them asking for more!

6 eggs, beaten
16.3-oz. tube refrigerated
  buttermilk biscuits
3 c. milk
6 T. all-purpose flour

salt and pepper to taste
1 lb. bacon, crisply cooked
  and crumbled
12-oz. pkg. shredded
  mozzarella cheese

Heat a lightly greased skillet over medium heat. Scramble eggs; cook just until set. Set aside. Press biscuits into the bottom of a greased 13"x9" baking pan to form a crust; press edges to seal. Bake at 350 degrees for 10 minutes; set aside to cool slightly. In a saucepan over medium-high heat, whisk together milk, flour, salt and pepper until well blended. Bring to a boil, stirring constantly until thickened. Pour hot mixture evenly over crust; layer scrambled eggs on top. Sprinkle with bacon and cheese. Bake an additional 10 to 15 minutes, or until cheese is bubbly. Serves 6.

Need an extra stocking? Fill a pair of vintage ice skates with tiny wrapped gifts or greenery to hang on the mantel.

Goldenrod Eggs

Fawn McKenzie
Wenatchee, WA

Goldenrod Eggs is an old family recipe that has been handed down from my Great-Grandmother Rhodes and my Great-Aunt Ruby. When our nieces were very small and couldn't say "Goldenrod" they called it Gravy Eggs. This has always been a comfort food as well as a great holiday breakfast.

5 to 6 eggs, hard-boiled, peeled
   and halved
6 T. butter or sausage drippings
6 T. all-purpose flour

2-3/4 c. to 3 c. milk
salt and pepper to taste
toast or split biscuits

Place egg yolks in a small bowl; mash and set aside. Chop whites and set aside. Place butter or drippings in a medium saucepan over medium-high heat; whisk in flour. Slowly pour in milk until desired consistency is achieved. Continue to heat through until mixture thickens. Stir in egg whites; season with salt and pepper as desired. Spoon over toast or biscuits. Sprinkle mashed egg yolks over each serving. Serves 4.

Turn a muffin tin into a terrific candy cup. Give it a fresh look with a light coat of snowy white spray paint, and when thoroughly dry, place paper liners in each cup. Filled with candies, these dressed-up muffin tins also make thoughtful hostess gifts.

Sausage Gravy for Biscuits

Sharon Crider
Junction City, KS

*Keep Christmas morning simple...dress up store-bought biscuits
with this delicious homestyle gravy.*

1 lb. sage-flavored ground pork sausage	1/2 t. poultry seasoning
2 T. onion, finely chopped	1/2 t. nutmeg
6 T. all-purpose flour	1/4 t. salt
1 qt. milk	4 to 6 biscuits, split

Crumble sausage into a large saucepan over medium-low heat. Add onion and cook, stirring often, until sausage is browned and onion is transparent. Drain, reserving 2 tablespoons drippings in saucepan. Stir in flour. Cook over medium-low heat about 6 minutes, or until mixture bubbles and becomes golden. Stir in milk and seasonings; cook and stir until thickened. To serve, spoon gravy over biscuit halves. Makes 4 to 6 servings.

Ribbon-covered buttons are so pretty when used to decorate packages, and covered-button kits can easily be found at craft or fabric stores. Simply wrap each button top with ribbon, then snap on the back. It's so easy!

Dutch Breakfast Cake

Leticia Weemhoff
Piedmont, OK

This is a fine recipe for a Sunday breakfast or brunch, first given to me by my husband's grandma when we were married. It came with her from the old country, where she learned to make this as a child. She's no longer with us but every time we have this cake, she's right there in our hearts.

4 c. all-purpose flour	2 eggs, beaten
3 c. sugar	1 c. milk
2 t. baking powder	1 t. vanilla extract
1 c. butter	

Whisk together flour, sugar and baking powder. Cut in butter until mixture resembles fine crumbs. Remove one cup of crumbs for topping; set aside. Whisk together eggs, milk and vanilla until smooth; add to flour mixture. Pour into three greased 8" round cake pans. Sprinkle reserved crumbs over batter. Bake at 350 degrees for 30 minutes, or until center tests done. Makes 3 cakes; each serves 5.

Small packages are a snap to wrap...just cover pint-size plain paint cans from the home center with festive holiday papers. Then fill cans with sweet treats, gift cards and other goodies.

Mocha Muffins

Paige Woodard
Loveland, CO

I first tasted these muffins at a brunch given by my mother, and knew right away that my husband would love them! I was right...topped with a creamy spread, they've become a must-have at all of our family brunches.

2 c. all-purpose flour
3/4 c. plus 1 T. sugar
2-1/2 t. baking powder
1 t. cinnamon
1/2 t. salt
1 c. milk
2 T. plus 1/2 t. instant coffee
  granules, divided

1/2 c. butter, melted
1 egg, beaten
1-1/2 t. vanilla extract, divided
1 c. mini semi-sweet chocolate
  chips, divided
1/2 c. cream cheese, softened

Whisk together flour, sugar, baking powder, cinnamon and salt in a large bowl. In a small bowl, stir milk and 2 tablespoons coffee granules until coffee is dissolved. Add butter, egg and vanilla; mix well. Stir into dry ingredients just until moistened. Fold in 3/4 cup chocolate chips. Fill greased or paper-lined muffin cups 2/3 full. Bake at 375 degrees for 17 to 20 minutes for regular muffins, or 13 to 15 minutes for mini muffins. Cool for 5 minutes before removing from pans to wire racks. In a food processor or blender, combine cream cheese and remaining vanilla, coffee granules and mini chocolate chips. Cover and process until well blended. Refrigerate spread until serving time. Serve spread on the side. Makes 16 regular or 36 mini muffins.

Especially in Christmas week
Temptation is so great to peek!
Now wouldn't it be much more fun
If shoppers carried things undone?
-John Farrar

27

Savory Chicken Brunch Bake

Angie Ellefson
Milton, WI

My mother-in-law gave me this recipe when my husband and I were first married. I began making it to share and soon everyone was asking for the recipe.

2 10-3/4 oz. cans cream of
   chicken soup
1 c. sour cream
pepper to taste
5 boneless, skinless chicken
   breasts, cooked and cut into
   bite-size pieces

2 sleeves round buttery
   crackers, finely crushed
1/2 c. butter, melted
2 T. poppy seed
1/4 t. garlic salt

In a large bowl, blend together soup and sour cream; season with pepper. Stir in chicken and set aside. Place cracker crumbs in a medium bowl; stir in melted butter, poppy seed and garlic salt. Spoon half the cracker mixture into the bottom of a greased 13"x9" baking pan. Layer on chicken mixture and top with remaining cracker mixture. Cover with aluminum foil and bake at 350 degrees for 30 minutes. Remove foil and bake an additional 10 minutes, until top is golden. Let stand for 10 minutes before serving. Serves 6 to 8.

Just for fun, slip brunch invitations inside woolly mittens, then deliver to friends & family.

Chili Relleno Squares

Lisa Williams
Longmont, CO

*This recipe was always requested for brunch during
our mom's group at church.*

7-oz. can whole or diced green
    chiles, drained
12-oz. pkg. shredded Colby
    cheese
12-oz. pkg. shredded Monterey
    Jack cheese

4 eggs, beaten
12-oz. can evaporated milk
2 T. all-purpose flour
16-oz. jar red or green salsa

Spread chiles in the bottom of a greased 13"x9" baking pan. Mix
cheeses together and spread over chiles. In a separate bowl, whisk
together eggs, evaporated milk and flour; pour over cheeses. Bake at
375 degrees for 30 minutes, or until top is golden. Spread salsa over
top and bake an additional 5 to 10 minutes. Makes 10 to 12 servings.

Adding a splash of ginger ale to orange, cranberry and
apple juice makes them extra-special for holiday mornings.

Sweet English Breakfast Porridge

Jenny Barnes
New Windsor, MD

A sprinkling of brown sugar and a drizzle of cream makes servings of porridge so yummy.

4 c. water
1 t. salt
2-1/2 c. quick-cooking oats, uncooked
3 T. butter
1/4 t. cinnamon

1/4 t. nutmeg
1 c. brown sugar, packed
1/4 c. maple syrup
1/2 c. sweetened condensed milk
Optional: additional maple syrup

Bring water and salt to a boil in a medium saucepan. Stir in oats; cook over medium heat for one minute, stirring constantly. Remove from heat. Add remaining ingredients except garnish and mix well. Spoon into 6 cereal bowls and top with additional syrup, if desired. Makes 6 servings.

A centerpiece that's as easy as 1-2-3. Arrange a greenery wreath in the center of the table, place a holiday plate in the wreath opening, then set a plump pillar candle on the plate and light.

Apricot Oat Breakfast

Stephanie Fackrell
Preston, ID

*This delicious recipe is from my mom. She wanted us to get
in the habit of eating a good breakfast, and would tell us,
"Breakfast-less children make unhealthy adults!"*

2 c. long-cooking oats,
  uncooked
1/3 c. slivered almonds
3/4 c. dried apricots, chopped
1/4 t. salt
1-1/2 c. orange juice

1 c. water
1/4 c. honey
Optional: milk
Garnish: chopped apricots,
  slivered almonds

Combine oats, nuts, dried apricots and salt together in a large bowl;
set aside. Whisk together orange juice, water and honey; add to oat
mixture. Refrigerate, covered, for 8 hours to overnight. Serve cold,
garnished as desired. Serves 4 to 6.

When decorating the Christmas tree, keep extra-special
ornaments at eye level and above. Then, place unbreakable
ornaments on lower branches...an ideal solution
for curious little ones and pets too!

Greek Stuffed Breakfast Loaf

Thomas Golden
Waverly, NY

While we love cooking, we really prefer spending our time enjoying our friends & family versus being tied to the kitchen. This recipe has become the staple breakfast dish at our home when company comes in. It can easily be prepared the evening before and simply needs to be baked the morning it is to be served. The flavors make the dish seem like it took hours to prepare...just keep our secret!

1 T. oil
1 doz. eggs, beaten
1 round loaf rye or sourdough
  bread
12-oz. pkg. baby spinach
12-oz. pkg. crumbled
  feta cheese

8-oz. can sliced mushrooms,
  drained
1 lb. ground pork breakfast
  sausage, cooked and drained

Heat oil in a large skillet over medium-low heat. Add eggs; cook and stir until set. Slice the top from bread; set aside. Hollow out inside of loaf, leaving approximately one inch of crust around the outside. Save bread pieces for another recipe. Layer half the spinach inside the bread loaf. Top spinach with half the feta cheese and all the mushrooms. Layer on sausage, scrambled eggs, remaining feta cheese and spinach. Place top back on loaf to cover and wrap tightly with aluminum foil. Bake at 375 degrees for approximately 45 minutes. Slice and serve hot. Makes 8 servings.

Old-fashioned favorites like a vintage sled or pair of ice skates by the front door are a sweet welcome for friends. Tie on evergreen boughs, pine cones & red berry sprigs for cheery color.

Spinach & Feta Pie

Leah-Anne Schnapp
Effort, PA

This is a great brunch meal...I usually serve a tossed salad filled with colorful veggies alongside. It truly tastes as if you spent all day making it, but it's as "easy as pie."

10-oz. pkg. frozen chopped
  spinach, thawed and drained
1/2 c. crumbled feta cheese
1/4 c. green onion, sliced
1/2 c. biscuit baking mix

2/3 c. milk
1/4 t. salt
1/8 t. pepper
2 eggs, beaten

Combine spinach, cheese and onion in a greased 9" pie plate. Stir together remaining ingredients until well blended; pour into pie plate. Bake at 400 degrees for 30 to 35 minutes, or until a knife tip inserted in center comes out clean. Let stand 5 minutes before slicing. Makes 6 to 8 servings.

Turn your holiday cards into a Christmas garland. Use mini clothespins to clip them to a length of ribbon, add some favorite holiday photos and handmade gift tags to create a heartfelt decoration that your family will enjoy all season long.

Cheese Strata

Andrina Thomas
Kent, WA

*Crisply cooked and crumbled bacon or browned sausage
would also taste great in this brunch favorite.*

8 slices bread
8-oz. pkg. shredded Cheddar
  cheese, divided
8-oz. pkg. shredded Swiss
  cheese, divided

1/4 c. green onion, chopped
pepper to taste
4 eggs, beaten
2 c. milk
2 T. butter, melted

Arrange 4 slices bread in a greased 13"x9" baking pan. Sprinkle one cup of each cheese over bread. Top with one tablespoon green onion; add pepper as desired. Repeat layering with remaining bread, cheeses, onion and pepper. Whisk eggs, milk and butter together. Pour evenly over layers. Cover tightly with aluminum foil and refrigerate at least 6 hours to overnight. Bake, uncovered, at 325 degrees for 40 minutes. Serve hot. Serves 4 to 6.

Everyone likes little surprises at Christmastime, so tuck a little something extra in holiday cards. A child's drawing or sprinkle of gold stars is sure to bring a smile.

Hearty Breakfast Bake

Ronda Wilson
Shenandoah Junction, WV

Add different ingredients to this recipe if you like...sometimes I'll toss in a little chopped green pepper or sliced mushrooms. My son Devan loves to top slices with maple syrup.

20-oz. pkg. refrigerated
   shredded hashbrowns
3/4 c. onion, diced
1-1/2 c. turkey ham, cubed
salt and pepper to taste

1/2 c. shredded Cheddar cheese
1/2 c. shredded mozzarella
   cheese
4 eggs, beaten
1 c. milk

In a greased 9"x9" baking pan, layer hashbrowns, onion and ham. Sprinkle with salt and pepper as desired. Top with cheeses. In a medium bowl, whisk eggs and milk; pour mixture over cheeses. Cover with aluminum foil and bake at 350 degrees for 20 minutes. Remove aluminum foil and continue baking another 5 to 10 minutes, or until golden. Cut into squares to serve. Makes 4 to 6 servings.

Placecards with whimsy...tie a ribbon around each guest's juice glass, then slip a tiny childhood snapshot under each ribbon!

Sunday Skillet Hash

Leianna Logan
Toledo, OH

This recipe conjures up some of my most favorite childhood memories. My mother always made this when we would head up north for a weekend at our cabin. It's simple to prepare and makes a hearty and delicious breakfast or brunch. I have often doubled this recipe, preparing it the night before and warming it in a slow cooker the next morning.

1 lb. ground pork sausage
2 lbs. potatoes, peeled and diced
1 onion, finely chopped
1 green pepper, finely chopped
salt and pepper to taste

Brown sausage in a large skillet; drain drippings. Stir in potatoes, onion and green pepper. Sprinkle with salt and pepper as desired. Cover and reduce heat to medium-low. Cook for 15 minutes, or until potatoes are fork-tender. Serves 4.

Set up a small tree in the kids' rooms...a great way
for them to show off homemade and favorite
ornaments of their very own.

Breakfast & Brunch with Friends

Maple Ham & Eggs Cups

Staci Meyers
Montezuma, GA

Great breakfast or brunch recipe...the kids will love it too.

1 T. butter, melted
6 slices deli ham
1 T. maple syrup
6 eggs

1 t. butter, cut into 6 pieces
salt and pepper to taste
toast, English muffins or
   biscuits

Brush muffin cups with melted butter; line each cup with a slice of ham. Pour 1/2 teaspoon maple syrup over each ham slice; top with one pat of butter. Crack one egg into each ham cup; season with salt and pepper as desired. Bake at 400 degrees for 20 minutes, or until eggs are set. Remove muffin tin from oven; use a spoon or gently twist each serving to loosen. Serve with toast, on English muffins or on split biscuits. Makes 6.

The mantel is always a favorite spot for hanging stockings, but for something new, hang them on bedposts... what a fun discovery Christmas morning!

Mom's Chocolate Gravy

Teresa Ward
Halls, TN

*My 2 girls love this chocolatey treat spooned over warm biscuits.
When their friends from school would sleep over,
this is what they wanted for breakfast.*

1 c. sugar
1-1/2 c. milk
1-1/2 T. all-purpose flour

2 T. baking cocoa
2 T. butter

Combine all ingredients in a small saucepan over medium heat. Cook and stir until desired consistency is reached. Makes 8 to 10 servings.

It's easy to turn an old wool sweater into the sweetest pint-size wreaths! Felt the sweater by setting the washing machine to a hot wash and a cold rinse, then toss in the dryer. Cut the felted wool into one-inch squares and push onto florists' wire that's shaped into a circle. A sweet little woolly wreath ready to use as a package topper.

Dandy Donut Muffins

Sandra Rivest
Enfield, CT

A cure for breakfast blahs!

1/3 c. shortening
1 c. sugar
1 egg, beaten
1-1/2 c. all-purpose flour
1-1/2 t. baking powder

1/4 t. nutmeg
1/2 c. milk
1/4 c. butter, melted
1/3 to 1/2 c. cinnamon-sugar

Using an electric mixer on medium speed, blend shortening and sugar until smooth; add egg and beat well. Whisk flour, baking powder and nutmeg together; blend in milk. Stir flour mixture into shortening mixture until well blended. Fill greased or paper-lined muffin cups 2/3 full. Bake at 350 degrees for 20 to 30 minutes, until golden. Remove muffins from tin and roll in melted butter; immediately toss in cinnamon-sugar. Makes 14.

Snow shovels are a must-have for snowy winters, and they also make fun welcome signs. Simply give the shovel 2 coats of chalkboard paint. Once dry, prop it by the door and write cheery greetings for friends, neighbors, even the letter carrier!

Festive Brunch Frittata

Renae Scheiderer
Beallsville, OH

This is a special recipe I like to make on Christmas morning.

8 eggs, beaten
1/2 t. salt
1/8 t. pepper
1/2 c. shredded Cheddar cheese
2 T. butter

2 c. red, green and yellow
   peppers, chopped
1/4 c. onion, chopped
Garnish: chopped fresh parsley

Beat together eggs, salt and pepper. Fold in cheese and set aside. Melt butter over medium heat in a 10" non-stick oven-safe skillet. Add peppers and onion to skillet; sauté until tender. Pour eggs over peppers and onion; don't stir. Cover and cook over medium-low heat for about 9 minutes. Eggs are set when frittata is lightly golden on the underside. Turn oven on broil. Move skillet from stovetop to oven; broil top about 5 inches from heat until lightly golden. Garnish with parsley. Serves 6.

No mantel for stockings?
An old-fashioned wooden
ladder can stand in
during the holidays!

40

Christmas Kitchen Casserole

Natalie Goulding
Wasilla, AK

This is one of my favorite breakfast recipes for Christmas. I even prepare it the night before so while we are opening our gifts, it bakes in the oven. This way, I can enjoy what Santa brought to our home!

20-oz. pkg. frozen shredded
   hashbrowns, thawed
4 green onions, chopped
8-oz. pkg. shredded Cheddar
   cheese

2 c. cooked ham, diced
1 T. green pepper, finely chopped
6 eggs, beaten
1/4 c. sour cream
1/4 c. milk

Layer hashbrowns, onions, cheese, ham and pepper in a greased 13"x9" baking pan. Whisk eggs with sour cream and milk. Pour mixture over layered ingredients. Bake, uncovered, at 400 degrees for 35 minutes. Remove from oven; cover with aluminum foil and return to oven for an additional 10 minutes. Serves 6 to 8.

Choose several colorful paint pens from the craft store and use them to add whimsical patterns, pictures and holiday greetings to plain glass ball ornaments.

Norwegian Pancakes

Lori Ritchey
Denver, PA

*Need something different or special for a holiday breakfast or
brunch? These pancakes are deliciously different!*

1/3 c. sour cream
1/3 c. cottage cheese
2 eggs, beaten
1/4 c. all-purpose flour
1 t. sugar

1/4 t. salt
15-oz. can sliced peaches
1 T. cinnamon
1 T. brown sugar, packed
Optional: whipped cream

In a medium bowl, combine sour cream and cottage cheese. Stir until
well blended. Add eggs, blending well. Whisk together flour, sugar
and salt; add to egg mixture. Pour batter onto a hot greased griddle by
1/4 cupfuls. When bubbles form around pancake edges, turn and cook
until other side is golden. Combine peaches, cinnamon and brown
sugar in a saucepan over medium heat; cook just until hot. Top each
pancake with a large spoonful of warm peaches. Add a dollop of
whipped cream, if desired. Serves 4 to 6.

Arrange holiday mugs, spoons, a couple of cinnamon sticks
and a favorite spiced cider recipe on a vintage
serving tray for a thoughtful gift.

A Warm
Holiday

Welcome

Quick Cheese Fondue

Rosemary Trezza
Tarpon Springs, FL

We love this recipe my sister shared with me. In fact, my grown children and I serve this appetizer at most get-togethers with our friends & family.

10-3/4 oz. can Cheddar cheese
   soup
1 c. French onion dip
1 c. shredded sharp Cheddar
   cheese

1/2 t. dry mustard
1/8 to 1/4 t. cayenne pepper
1 loaf French bread, cubed

Combine all ingredients except bread cubes in a medium saucepan, stirring well to blend. Place saucepan over low heat until cheese has melted, stirring constantly. Serve with bread cubes for dipping. Makes 6 servings.

A fondue pot is a must for keeping savory or sweet dipping sauces just right for serving. Simply fill the fondue pot, turn it to the warm setting and forget about it!

Cheesy Cocktail Swirls

Michelle Campen
Peoria, IL

I love to make these quick & easy appetizers.

8-oz. tube refrigerated crescent
   rolls
3-oz. pkg. cream cheese,
   softened
2 T. onion, finely chopped

1 t. milk
5 slices bacon, crisply cooked
   and crumbled
1 T. grated Parmesan cheese

Separate dough into 4 rectangles; firmly press perforations to seal. Set aside. In a small bowl, blend cream cheese, onion and milk well. Spread 2 tablespoons cream cheese mixture evenly over each rectangle; sprinkle with bacon. Roll up, starting at longest side; pinch edges to seal. Cut each roll into 8 slices. Place slices on an ungreased baking sheet; sprinkle with Parmesan cheese. Bake at 375 degrees for 12 to 15 minutes, until golden. Makes about 2-1/2 dozen.

Cookie cutters, shortbread cookies and sparkly
ornaments tied up with ribbon look so
festive hanging in kitchen windows.

Toss-it-Together Salsa

Aaron Martelli
Santa Fe, TX

As my wife can tell you, I am a "throw it together" type of guy.
I was hungry one night for salsa and chips and tossed these
ingredients together. It turned out to be a winner!

2 14-1/2 oz. cans petite diced   1 t. garlic, chopped
   tomatoes   1/3 c. pickled jalapeños, minced
1 onion, diced   salt and pepper to taste

Combine all ingredients in a small bowl; stir well. Serve immediately
or, if preferred, chill overnight. Makes 16 servings.

Family favorites like homemade salsa,
jams & jellies are perfect hostess gifts...
simply tie on a bow and gift tag!

Best-Ever Taco Cups

Ellen Nutter
Stanton, NE

So easy to prepare, you'll find yourself making these all the time.

1 lb. ground beef
1-1/4 oz. pkg. taco seasoning
   mix

12-oz. tube refrigerated
   buttermilk biscuits
1/2 c. shredded Cheddar cheese

Brown ground beef in a medium skillet over medium heat; drain. Add seasoning mix and prepare as directed on package. Set aside. Press biscuit dough into bottoms and up sides of muffin cups; fill with seasoned beef. Bake at 400 degrees for 15 minutes. Sprinkle with cheese; return to oven and bake an additional 2 to 3 minutes or until cheese is melted. Makes 10 to 20 servings.

Come on Over

Invite neighbors over for an afternoon holiday get-together.
Serve lots of easy-to-make appetizers, punch and sparkling
cider. Keeping it casual and fuss-free means you have
lots of time to catch up on each other's holiday plans.

Fruit & Nut Cheese Log

Sharon Demers
Dolores, CO

This recipe is one that is frequently requested when an appetizer is needed. It's very simple, yet so tasty as the cream cheese, fruit and chives give it a unique flavor.

8-oz. pkg. cream cheese,
  softened
1 T. apple jelly
1/4 c. dried apricots, chopped
1/4 c. dried tart cherries,
  chopped

1/4 c. chopped walnuts
Garnish: minced fresh chives
wheat crackers or fresh fruit

Place cream cheese on a sheet of plastic wrap; top with a second sheet of plastic wrap. Use a rolling pin to roll cheese to 1/2-inch thickness, approximately an 8-inch by 6-inch rectangle. Remove top sheet of plastic wrap and discard. Spread jelly over cheese; sprinkle with dried fruits. Gently roll into a log, jelly-roll style. Roll log in chopped walnuts and wrap in plastic wrap; refrigerate until ready to serve. Just before serving, sprinkle chives over log. Serve with wheat crackers and fresh fruit. Makes 8 to 10 servings.

Colorful felted wool mittens filled with greenery sprigs and bright berries make sweet place settings. Stitch buttons of all sizes & shapes around the cuffs for added whimsy!

Jezebel Sauce

Beckie Apple
Grannis, AR

I have three brothers and two sisters, and a few days before Christmas we gather our families together and spend time at Mom & Dad's to celebrate. We always enjoy a mix of old and new recipes, and this is one of the non-traditional appetizers we've come to really love.

18-oz. jar blackberry jam
18-oz. jar raspberry jam
1-1/2 oz. container dry mustard
5-oz. jar prepared horseradish
1/4 t. cayenne pepper

1 T. pepper
12-oz. container whipped
   cream cheese
toasted bread slices or
   buttery crackers

Combine all ingredients except cream cheese and bread or crackers in a medium bowl. Stir well and set aside 30 minutes. When ready to serve, spoon cream cheese onto a serving plate; spoon jam mixture over cream cheese. Serve with toasted bread slices or buttery crackers. Sauce may be refrigerated for up to 3 months. Makes 12 to 16 servings.

Découpage photos onto a package
for one-of-a-kind giftwrap!

Sweet-Hot Walnuts

Shelley Turner
Boise, ID

My brother Dan is a fabulous cook. On a recent visit to his Colorado ranch, he whipped up these spicy nuts in no time at all... we couldn't stop eating them!

1 c. walnut halves
1/4 t. cayenne pepper

1/4 c. sugar
1/8 t. salt

Combine all ingredients in a small skillet and mix well. Cook over medium heat, shaking skillet constantly, until sugar melts and ingredients are well blended. Pour onto a greased baking sheet; set aside to cool. Chop or break into small pieces. Makes about one cup.

Sing we all merrily Christmas is here,
The day we love best of all days in the year.
Bring forth the holly, the box and the bay,
Deck out our cottage for glad Christmas day.
-Old English poem

Honeyed Fruit Juice

Brenda Smith
Delaware, OH

Coming in from ice skating on a frozen lake in Maine, we were chilled to the bone. Little did we know Mom had put this wonderful juice blend in the slow cooker before we left...it was perfect.

64-oz. bottle cranberry-apple
   juice cocktail
2 c. apple juice
1 c. pomegranate juice
2/3 c. honey
1/2 c. orange juice
3 4-inch cinnamon sticks
10 whole cloves
2 T. orange zest

Combine the first 5 ingredients in a slow cooker. Wrap cinnamon sticks and cloves in a double thickness of cheesecloth; bring up corners of cloth and tie with kitchen string to form a bag. Add to slow cooker along with zest. Cover and cook on low setting for one to 2 hours. Discard spice bag before serving. Makes 3 quarts.

A warm-you-to-your-toes thermos of chocolatey cocoa
or warm spiced cider is a thoughtful neighbor gift...
perfect for frosty mornings!

Sun-Dried Tomato Toasties

*Lisanne Miller
Canton, MS*

*This recipe was the answer to a challenge among girlfriends...
develop an appetizer with five ingredients or less!*

1/2 c. sun-dried tomato and
   olive relish
2-1/4 oz. can chopped black
   olives, drained
2 t. garlic, chopped

8-oz. pkg. shredded mozzarella
   cheese, divided
1 loaf French bread, thinly
   sliced

Mix together first 3 ingredients and 1/4 cup cheese; spread evenly on
slices of bread. Arrange bread on an ungreased baking sheet; sprinkle
bread with remaining cheese. Bake at 300 degrees until cheese melts;
serve immediately. Makes 2 to 3 dozen.

A cheery, painted chalkboard is ideal for kids as they
count down the days until Christmas.

Caesar Toast Appetizers

Gladys Kielar
Perrysburg, OH

Crispy, savory bites ready in no time at all.

1 egg, beaten
1/4 c. Caesar salad dressing
8-oz. tube refrigerated crescent
  rolls

2 c. herb-flavored stuffing mix,
  crushed
1/3 c. grated Parmesan cheese

Mix egg and salad dressing in a small bowl; set aside. Unroll crescent roll dough and separate into 8 triangles. Cut each triangle of dough in half lengthwise, making 16 triangles. Dip triangles in egg mixture, then place in crushed stuffing to coat both sides. Place coated triangles one inch apart on an ungreased baking sheet. Sprinkle with Parmesan cheese. Bake at 375 degrees for 15 minutes. Makes 16.

A length of wire makes it easy to secure evergreen branches to a mailbox. Use chenille stems to wire on berry bunches and a bow, then tuck in a surprise for the letter carrier!

Diane's Delish Guacamole

Diane Stout
Zeeland, MI

Homemade guacamole is so much better than anything you can buy at the store. And with only four ingredients, it's oh-so simple to make.

2 avocados, pitted, peeled
  and mashed
1 t. lemon juice

1/3 c. to 1/2 c. medium-hot
  chunky salsa
salt and pepper to taste

Combine avocados, lemon juice, salsa, salt and pepper in a medium bowl; blend well. Makes 1-1/2 cups.

Create super teacher gifts in a jiffy. Dip clear ornaments into bright white latex paint and dust with mica snow. Slip the ornament hanger in place, then hang to dry.

Texas Green Sauce

Sandy Gay
Pittsburg, TX

I like to serve this with bean chalupas as well as tortilla chips.

4 avocados, pitted, peeled and
    chopped
16-oz. container sour cream
10-oz. can tomatoes with chiles
1 T. garlic powder

4-oz. can green chiles
2 t. salt
1 t. lemon juice
3-oz. pkg. cream cheese,
    softened

Combine all ingredients in an electric blender; process until smooth.
Makes 5 cups.

Winter is a fun-filled, magical time of year...make
snow angels, go sledding, even try ice skating!
A wintry bonfire with food, family & friends
will make it a time to remember.

Chinese Chicken Wings

Trisha Donley
Pinedale, WY

This is a very easy recipe, a quick go-to that's so yummy.
This appetizer can also be substituted with chicken drummies.

1/2 c. soy sauce
1/2 c. brown sugar, packed
1/2 c. margarine

1/4 c. water
1/2 t. dry mustard
4 lbs. chicken wings

Combine all ingredients except wings in a saucepan; cook for
5 minutes over medium heat. Place wings on an ungreased large
shallow baking pan; brush with sauce. Bake at 350 degrees for
one hour, turning occasionally and brushing with sauce. Makes
20 servings.

Oh-so easy...give personalized tea towels to friends & family.
Position a stencil on the towel and use a medium
brush to apply 2 coats of washable fabric paint.
Remove the stencil and set aside to dry.

Bacon Quesadillas

Edward Kielar
Perrysburg, OH

These yummy appetizers have zing...what flavor!

1 c. shredded Colby Jack cheese
1/4 c. bacon bits
1/4 c. green onion, thinly sliced
Optional: 4-oz. can green chiles

Optional: 1/4 c. red or green
   pepper, chopped
4 6-inch flour tortillas
Garnish: sour cream, salsa

Combine cheese, bacon bits and onion in a small bowl; add chiles and peppers, if desired. Sprinkle mixture equally over each tortilla. Fold tortillas in half; press lightly to seal edges. Arrange on a lightly greased baking sheet. Bake at 400 degrees for 8 to 10 minutes, until edges are lightly golden. Top with a dollop of sour cream and salsa. Makes 4 servings.

Line a vintage pail with a kitchen towel, tuck in some
freshly baked breadsticks and a bottle of dipping oil.
Deliver to a neighbor at dinnertime.

Santa Claus Cranberry Punch

Michelle Campen
Peoria, IL

A fruity punch the jolly old elf just might like more than milk & cookies!

2 c. cranberries
2 c. water
1 c. sugar
juice of 3 lemons

juice of 1 lime
1 qt. ginger ale, chilled
Garnish: red and green
   maraschino cherries

Cook berries, water and sugar in a medium saucepan over medium heat until berries burst. Set aside to cool; strain and discard pulp, reserving juice mixture. Combine juice mixture in a pitcher with lemon and lime juices; chill. At serving time, gently stir in ginger ale. Garnish servings with cherries. Makes 6 to 8 servings.

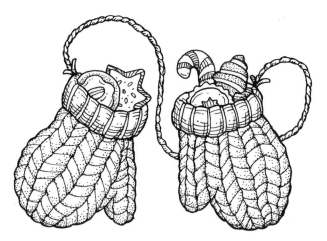

For a clever gift bag, tuck goodies inside a big woolly mitten.

Bacon-Wrapped Chestnuts

Deborah Smith
Milwaukee, WI

Every Christmas Eve my family has our own special party. We have candlelight, elegant appetizers, seafood and champagne all served on our best china and crystal. There is only one ticket of admission...you must arrive in your brand new Christmas pajamas! One favorite appetizer that we serve every year is bacon-wrapped chestnuts, this is our favorite recipe for them.

1/4 c. soy sauce
2 T. sugar
2 5-oz. cans water chestnuts,
   drained

10 slices bacon, halved

Combine soy sauce and sugar in a small bowl; stir in water chestnuts. Refrigerate chestnuts overnight to marinate. To prepare, wrap a bacon slice around each chestnut; secure with a wooden pick. Place on a rack in an ungreased shallow baking pan. Bake at 350 degrees for 30 to 35 minutes. Serve hot. Makes 10 servings.

Bring a bit of retro to the holiday kitchen...
tie on a vintage Christmas apron!

Holiday Stuffed Mushrooms

Jennifer Apthorpe
Panama, NY

I started making this recipe as a newlywed and it soon became one of my signature appetizers. My husband's grandfather especially wanted to know if I would be bringing them for our holiday dinner. The first time Grandpa tried them, he told Grandma not to leave before she got my recipe. Now every holiday when I make these special mushrooms, I think of Grandpa Morton and how much he liked them!

1 lb. bacon, crisply cooked
    and crumbled
8-oz. pkg. cream cheese,
    softened

1 T. dried, minced onion
2 t. Worcestershire sauce
1 lb. mushrooms, stems
    removed

With an electric mixer set to medium-high speed, thoroughly combine cream cheese, onion and Worcestershire sauce. Stir in bacon; fill mushroom caps with mixture. Arrange on an ungreased baking sheet. Bake at 375 degrees for 15 minutes, or until tops of mushrooms are golden. Makes 6 to 8 servings.

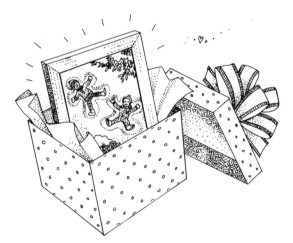

Slip a fun photo inside a frame...a terrific gift
that's sure to be appreciated.

Almond-Bacon Spread

Joan Clark
Cortland, OH

This is a very old recipe that I've used for many years.

1/4 c. roasted almonds, finely
  chopped
2 slices bacon, crisply cooked
  and crumbled
1 c. shredded American cheese

1 T. green onion, chopped
1/2 c. mayonnaise
1/8 t. salt
crackers or sliced party rye

Stir together all ingredients except crackers or bread in a medium bowl until thoroughly combined. Spoon into a crock or serving bowl. Serve with crackers or sliced party rye. Makes 6 servings.

A vintage muffin tin is perfect for serving a variety
of savory spreads. Just spoon a different
spread into each muffin cup.

Herbed Bread Chips

Geneva Rogers
Gillette, WY

A delicious snack...either by themselves or with a savory dip.

1 loaf French bread, sliced
   1/8-inch thick
1/2 c. butter, melted
1 t. dried parsley
1 t. dried rosemary

1 t. dried thyme
1 t. garlic powder
1/2 t. dried sage
1/4 t. salt

Place bread slices in a large bowl; set aside. Mix remaining ingredients in a small bowl. Pour over bread, tossing well to coat. Arrange bread on a lightly greased baking sheet. Bake at 300 degrees for 40 minutes, stirring occasionally, until crisp and golden. May be stored up to 2 weeks in an airtight container. Makes 1-1/2 dozen.

Empty jam jars filled with old-fashioned sweets like hard candies and gumdrops make thoughtful gifts. Cover the lid of each jar with a piece of fabric cut with pinking shears and tied on with a pretty ribbon.

Feta Cheese Ball

Anne Richey
Syracuse, IN

This is not your typical cheese ball...it's a great twist on an old favorite. Easily doubled, I make it often for family & friends.

8-oz. container crumbled feta
  cheese
8-oz. pkg. cream cheese,
  softened

2 T. butter, softened
1 T. fresh dill weed, chopped
1 clove garlic, minced
assorted crackers

Combine all ingredients except crackers. Beat with an electric mixer on low speed. When well blended, form cheese mixture into a ball and wrap in plastic wrap. Refrigerate at least 4 hours or overnight. Serve with assorted crackers. Makes 8 to 10 servings.

For a simple, sweetly scented place setting, tie a few cinnamon sticks together with raffia, attach a mailing label as a name card and lay a bundle across each plate.

Salmon Loaf Dip

Suzanne Morley
Kent, England

*My most requested recipe...friends can't stop eating it
and always ask for the recipe.*

1 large loaf crusty bread
1 onion, finely chopped
1 to 2 t. oil
8-oz. pkg. cream cheese,
  softened
2 7-3/4 oz. cans salmon,
  drained

3 to 4 T. sour cream
1 t. hot pepper sauce
1/8 t. salt
1/8 t. pepper
1 t. fresh dill weed, chopped

Slice the top from bread loaf. Hollow out center, tearing bread into cubes; set aside. Sauté onion with oil in a medium saucepan. When onion is soft, place in a medium bowl; blend in remaining ingredients. Spoon mixture into hollow loaf; replace bread lid and place on an ungreased baking sheet. Bake at 350 degrees for 30 minutes. Add reserved bread cubes to baking sheet; bake both for an additional 30 minutes. Serve dip with warmed bread cubes. Makes 4 to 8 servings.

It's easy to craft a personalized ornament that's ready in no time at all. Apply rub-on letters, found in a scrapbooking store, to plain ornaments...finish off with a ribbon.

Warm Gorgonzola Dip

Corinne Gross
Tigard, OR

*I received this recipe from a dear friend and whenever I serve
this dip I'm always asked for the recipe.*

1-1/4 c. whipping cream
1/4 t. garlic, minced
1/4 t. dried thyme

1/3 c. crumbled Gorgonzola
cheese

Combine cream, garlic and thyme in a small saucepan; bring to a boil
over medium-low heat. Add cheese and whisk until cheese melts.
Reduce heat to low, stirring occasionally. Simmer gently, until it is
reduced by half. Sauce will thicken as it reduces. Serve with warm
Garlic Cheese Bread. Serves 6.

Garlic Cheese Bread:

1/2 c. butter, softened
1/2 c. grated Parmesan cheese
1-1/2 t. garlic, minced
3/4 t. dried basil

3/4 t. dried oregano
1 loaf French bread, halved
lengthwise

In a small bowl, combine all ingredients except bread. Spread over
each half of bread. Place bread halves on a baking sheet and broil
until golden, about 3 to 5 minutes.

Sweet & Sour Meatballs

Becky Stewart
Alliance, OH

Great bite-size appetizers or enjoy for meatball sandwiches.

12-oz. jar chili sauce
16-oz. can cranberry sauce
2 T. brown sugar, packed

2-lb. pkg. frozen Italian
   meatballs

In a medium saucepan, combine chili sauce, cranberry sauce and brown sugar. Cook over medium heat until warm. Place meatballs into a slow cooker; coat with sauce mixture. Cover and cook on high setting until heated through, about 2 hours, or on low setting for about 6 hours. Makes 10 to 15 servings.

Arrange tall veggies like carrot sticks, celery and asparagus in skinny drinking glasses...so simple and creative.

Creamy Raspberry Spread

Susann Kropp
East Durham, NY

A food processor makes easy work of this recipe.

1 lb. Cheddar cheese, cubed
1 onion, chopped and divided
1 clove garlic
3/4 c. mayonnaise

1/2 t. hot pepper sauce
1/2 c. chopped pecans
1 c. raspberry preserves
crackers

In a food processor, place 1/4 each of cheese, onion and garlic. Process until finely minced. Gradually add remaining cheese and onion alternating with mayonnaise. Add hot sauce and continue to blend. Transfer mixture to a medium bowl; stir in pecans. Spoon mixture in a ring on a serving plate and chill in refrigerator overnight. Before serving, spoon raspberry preserves into center of ring. Serve with crackers. Makes 50 servings.

Have a holiday movie marathon! Toss pillows and quilts on the floor, set out lots of snacks and have a non-stop viewing of all the best Christmas movies.

Caramel Popcorn

Laurie Lotto
Green Bay, WI

*This is a Christmas favorite at my house. It takes a little time
but the wait is worth it....the popcorn melts in your mouth.*

12 c. popped popcorn
Optional: 1 c. chopped nuts
1 c. butter
1 c. dark corn syrup

1-1/2 c. sugar
1 t. vanilla extract
1/2 t. baking soda

Arrange popcorn and nuts, if using, on a jelly-roll pan. Place in oven
at 200 degrees to keep warm while preparing caramel. In a medium
saucepan over medium heat, blend together butter, syrup and sugar.
Cook and stir until mixture comes to a rolling boil; boil 5 minutes
longer. Stir in vanilla and baking soda; continue to heat until mixture
foams. Remove from heat and immediately pour caramel over popcorn,
stirring until well coated. Bake for one hour at 250 degrees, stirring
every 15 minutes. Remove from oven; spread on sheets of wax paper
to cool. Store in an airtight container. Makes 12 to 15 servings.

Fill a tall glass bowl with pearly white ornaments...
oh-so-pretty on a buffet table or mantel.

White Chocolate Party Mix

Lecia Stevenson
Timberville, VA

My sister, Lena Phillips, is always making the most delicious snacks for Christmas. I ask for the recipes and they are always fast and easy. She gave me this mix one year for a Christmas gift. I totally enjoyed it and now make it myself.

5 c. doughnut-shaped oat cereal
5 c. bite-size crispy corn cereal squares
10-oz. pkg. mini pretzel twists
2 c. salted peanuts

16-oz. pkg. candy-coated chocolates
2 12-oz. pkgs. white chocolate chips
3 T. oil

Combine first 5 ingredients in a large bowl; set aside. In a microwave-safe bowl, heat white chocolate chips and oil on medium-high setting for 2 minutes, stirring once. Continue to microwave on high for 10 seconds; stir until smooth. Pour over cereal mixture and stir well to coat. Spread onto 3 wax paper-lined baking sheets. Break apart when cool. Store in an airtight container. Makes 5 quarts.

Turn a pair of snowshoes into a wintertime memo board. Search out barn sales for a pair of matching snowshoes, dust them off and hang on the wall. It's easy to clip wish lists, shopping lists and photos to the webbing with paper clips or mini clothespins.

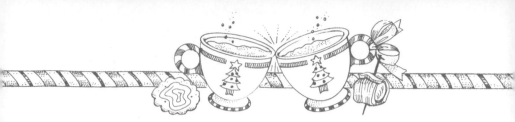

Country Cocoa

Sharon Crider
Junction City, KS

When you're in the mood for a cup of creamy cocoa,
this is the perfect recipe.

1 c. milk
1 T. sugar
1 T. baking cocoa

1/2 t. vanilla extract
1 marshmallow

In a microwave-safe 2-cup glass measure, combine milk, sugar, cocoa and vanilla. Microwave 3 to 3-1/2 minutes, stirring after one minute. Pour into a mug and top with a marshmallow. Makes one cup.

Vermont Eggnog

Tina Wright
Atlanta, GA

My sister lives in Vermont and she's always looking for ways to use maple syrup. This is one of her best recipes...so quick & easy too.

32-oz. container eggnog, chilled
1/2 c. maple syrup

Garnish: whipped cream, nutmeg

In a one-quart pitcher, combine eggnog and maple syrup. Refrigerate until chilled. Before serving, stir eggnog; pour into individual glasses. Garnish servings with whipped cream and nutmeg. Makes one quart.

Creamy cocoa is extra special
when mugs are topped with
a chocolate cookie...yum!

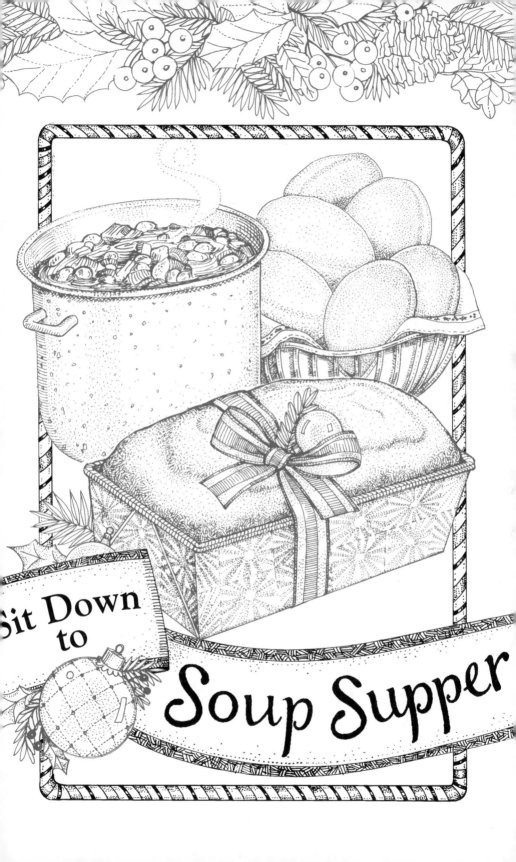

Sit Down to Soup Supper

Bean with Bacon Soup

Katie Aguilera
Prairie Village, KS

My Grandma Ginger would always make a similar version of this soup for me when I was little. This is my re-creation of that soup, a little more grown-up, but still with the same memories.

1/4 lb. bacon, crisply cooked, crumbled and 2 T. drippings reserved
1 to 2 T. butter
1/2 red onion, finely chopped
1/2 red pepper, finely chopped
1 carrot, peeled and finely chopped
3 cloves garlic, minced
salt and pepper to taste

1 t. fresh thyme, minced
1/4 c. dry white wine or chicken broth
2 T. all-purpose flour
2 c. chicken broth
15-oz. can Great Northern beans, drained and rinsed
Garnish: grated Parmesan cheese

Place reserved drippings in a stockpot. Add butter, onion, red pepper and carrot. Sauté over medium heat until vegetables are tender. Stir in garlic; cook for about 2 minutes. Sprinkle with salt and pepper. Stir in thyme; cook for one minute. Add wine or broth; continue to cook over medium heat until liquid evaporates. Whisk in flour; cook for 2 minutes. Stir in broth; simmer for 2 to 3 minutes. Stir in beans and reserved bacon; cook until heated through. Sprinkle with cheese. Makes 2 to 4 servings.

It's easy to keep rolls nice and warm alongside servings of soup. Before arranging rolls in a bread basket, place a terra cotta warming tile in the bottom and line with a Christmasy tea towel.

White Bean & Sausage Stew

Diane Cohen
Breinigsville, PA

So filling, this makes a warming soup supper.

6 Italian pork sausage links
1/4 c. water
1 T. olive oil
1 onion, chopped
1 clove garlic, chopped
2 15-oz. cans Great Northern
   beans, drained and rinsed

28-oz. can chopped tomatoes,
   drained
1 t. dried thyme
salt and pepper to taste

Pierce sausages with a fork; place in a large non-stick skillet. Add water; bring to a boil over medium heat. Reduce heat to low; simmer for 10 minutes, turning occasionally, until water evaporates and sausages are browned. Transfer to a plate. Heat oil in skillet over medium-high heat. Add onion and garlic; cook, stirring often, about 3 minutes. Add beans, tomatoes and thyme. Transfer half of bean mixture to a slow cooker; arrange sausages on top. Spread remaining bean mixture over sausages. Cover and cook on high setting for 2 hours. Stir in additional water, if needed. Remove sausages; slice thickly and return to slow cooker for 2 additional hours. Sprinkle with salt and pepper. Serves 4.

Tree trimming is more fun with family & friends. Put a big pot of soup on the stove to simmer, and by the time the tree topper is in place, it'll be time to sit down and enjoy dinner together.

Cream of Tomato Soup

Tyson Ann Trecannelli
Falling Waters, WV

Filled with chicken, this is a nice hearty soup and especially great with grilled cheese sandwiches or crusty rolls. I always make this soup when we get our first frost...it just makes the whole house smell so warm and cozy. I created this recipe several years ago as an alternative to just plain tomato soup, and I always hear, "Tastes like MORE!"

2 10-3/4 oz. cans tomato soup
4 c. chicken broth
14-1/2 oz. can diced tomatoes
1/2 c. brown or white
   long-cooking rice, uncooked
2 T. olive oil
1-1/2 c. cooked chicken,
   chopped

2 T. dried parsley
1 T. dried basil
2 T. butter
1/4 to 1/3 c. whipping cream or
   half-and-half

Combine all ingredients except butter and cream or half-and-half in a medium stockpot. Simmer, stirring occasionally, over medium-low heat for about one hour and 15 minutes. Add butter; stir to melt. Blend in cream or half-and-half just before serving. Serves 6 to 8.

A sweet placecard friends can take home. Write each friend's name on a vintage Christmas postcard, then clip onto the side of a plate.

Perfect Rolls

Lauren Williams
Kewanee, MO

My aunt gave me this recipe...these rolls are truly perfect every time. I adapted it to use the rapid-rise yeast so they're ready in half the time.

1 env. rapid-rise yeast
4 c. all-purpose flour
1/2 c. sugar
1 t. salt

1/2 c. oil
1 c. hot water, 110 to 115 degrees
2 eggs, beaten

Whisk together yeast, flour, sugar and salt in a large bowl. Pour oil into a bowl; slowly pour hot water over oil. Stir to blend. Add eggs to flour mixture; blend well. Stir in oil mixture. Continue to stir until mixture is smooth. Cover and set aside for 10 minutes. If dough is sticky, knead in enough additional flour until dough is easy to handle. Roll out dough on a lightly floured surface to one-inch thickness. Cut with a biscuit cutter and place on an ungreased baking sheet. Cover and let dough rise for 3 to 4 hours or until double in bulk. Bake at 375 degrees for 15 minutes, or until golden. Makes one dozen.

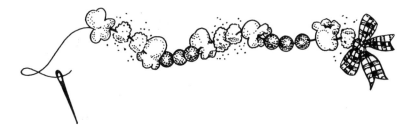

Enjoy some family fun like Grandma used to have...stringing popcorn and cranberries together! The kids will love it, and the strands are so pretty draped along a mantel, doorway and, of course, on the Christmas tree!

Minted Green Bean Salad

Jo Ann
Gooseberry Patch

A very good bean salad...I love the fresh herb flavors
and wine vinegar dressing.

3/4 lb. green beans, trimmed
1/2 t. garlic, minced
1/4 t. salt
2 T. white wine vinegar
1 T. lemon juice

salt and pepper to taste
2 T. olive oil
1 T. fresh mint, minced
1/2 T. fresh basil, minced
1/4 c. red onion, finely chopped

In a stockpot of boiling water, cook beans for 3 to 5 minutes, or until crisp-tender. Transfer beans to a large bowl of ice water to chill; drain well. Combine garlic and salt in a small bowl. Use the back of a spoon to crush garlic to the consistency of paste. Add vinegar, lemon juice, salt and pepper to taste; whisk to blend. Add oil and herbs; whisk until well blended. In a bowl combine together beans and onion; tossing with dressing to coat. Chill 20 minutes before serving. Makes 2 servings.

Hollowed-out mini loaves of round bread are just right
for individual servings of soups, stews and salads. Bigger
loaves of bread can even be hollowed out and filled with
salads to serve 'round the table family style.
And the best part...no dishes to wash!

Cabin Salad

Vicki Channer
Fairview Heights, IL

There's a restaurant down the road in what used to be a pioneer cabin. My mom and I love the salad they serve so much, that we began tweaking recipes to create our own version. We came up with this recipe, so now we can have this delicious salad whenever we want!

1 c. sugar
2 t. paprika
2 t. dry mustard
2 t. celery seed
2 T. dried, minced onion
2 t. salt
1/4 t. pepper
1 c. oil

1/2 c. vinegar
1 head lettuce, chopped
5-oz. can sliced water chestnuts, drained
3-oz. jar bacon bits
14-oz. can bean sprouts, drained
9-oz. pkg. baby spinach

Whisk together first 7 ingredients in a medium bowl until well blended. Spoon into a one-quart jar. Add oil and vinegar to jar; tighten lid and shake until mixture is thoroughly combined. In a large bowl, toss together lettuce, water chestnuts, bacon bits, bean sprouts and spinach. Pour desired amount of dressing over salad; toss well before serving. Serves 4.

Fill a garden bell jar with clementines, pomegranates and shiny green apples. Cover the opening with a plate and turn right-side up. A centerpiece in no time at all!

Sobi's Cabbage Chowda

Connie Poliquin
Raymond, NH

My brother-in-law, Joe, opened a restaurant in New Hampshire, and soon became known for his home-cooked New England fare. At one family get-together, he and his step-son, Ricky, created this delicious soup that quickly became a must-have!

2 c. potatoes, peeled and cut
  into bite-size pieces
2 c. carrots, peeled and cut into
  bite-size pieces
1 c. cabbage, shredded
1 c. onion, shredded
2 c. Kielbasa, chopped

2 14-oz. cans cream of
  celery soup
14-1/2 oz. can beef or
  chicken broth
salt and pepper to taste
1-3/4 c. milk

Combine all ingredients except milk in a stockpot over medium heat. Bring to a boil. Reduce heat and stir in milk. Simmer for 20 to 30 minutes, until heated through. Makes 4 to 6 servings.

A basket filled with warm & cozy blankets sitting alongside a stack of favorite holiday stories will invite little ones to snuggle in for bedtime stories.

Wild Rice & Mushroom Soup

Jennifer Niemi
Nova Scotia, Canada

Once leftovers are refrigerated, this soup will become thicker.
You'll want to add additional vegetable broth when reheating.

4 c. water
2 t. salt
1 c. wild rice, uncooked
3 T. olive oil
4 c. onion, finely chopped
10 c. vegetable broth, divided

3 cloves garlic, minced
1/2 c. brown rice, uncooked
1/8 t. pepper
1/3 c. sherry or vegetable broth
4 c. mushrooms, thinly sliced

Combine water and salt in a large saucepan over medium-high heat; bring to a boil. Add wild rice and simmer, covered, for 35 minutes. Drain and rinse wild rice well under cold water; set aside. Heat oil in a skillet over medium heat; cook onion for 10 minutes, or until softened and translucent. Add 6 cups broth, garlic and brown rice. Simmer, covered, for 20 minutes. Stir in pepper, sherry or broth, prepared wild rice, mushrooms and remaining broth. Simmer, uncovered, 15 minutes. Makes 6 servings.

It's fun to hang little unexpected surprises from the dining room chandelier. Start with a swag of greenery, then tuck in Christmas whimsies like glass balls, tiny snowmen, cookie cutters and smiling Santas.

Christmas Cherry Salad

Lois Kiser
Santa Maria, CA

An refreshing salad that's a perfect addition to any meal.

1 c. cherry pie filling
3-oz. pkg. cherry gelatin mix
3/4 c. cola

8-oz. can crushed pineapple,
   drained
Optional: 1/4 t. almond extract

Bring cherry pie filling to a boil in a saucepan over medium heat.
Add gelatin mix; stir until dissolved. Remove from heat; stir in cola,
pineapple and almond extract, if using. Pour into a 4-cup gelatin mold
or serving dish. Refrigerate until set, about 8 hours, or overnight.
Unmold onto a chilled serving platter. Serves 10 to 12.

Loosen a chilled salad from the mold in a snap.
Dip the bottom of the mold in warm water.
Set a plate over the top of the mold and turn
right-side up...the salad should slip out easily!

Sit Down to Soup Supper

Family Pineapple Salad

Barbara Ginney
Clermont, FL

This recipe was passed down from my mother to me about 40 years ago. My two daughters have now joined in on the tradition of preparing it for their families. It is easy to make...I really should make it more often!

1/4 c. cold water
1 env. unflavored gelatin
3/4 c. sugar
8-oz. can crushed pineapple,
    drained and juice reserved

1 c. whipping cream
1 c. cottage cheese
5 maraschino cherries, halved

Pour water into a medium bowl; stir in gelatin until dissolved. Set aside. Pour sugar into a 2-quart saucepan; add reserved pineapple juice. Heat over medium-low heat until sugar has dissolved. Remove from heat and stir into gelatin mixture. Set aside until mixture is room temperature. With an electric mixer on high speed, beat whipping cream until stiff peaks form. Add pineapple and cottage cheese to cooled gelatin mixture. Fold in whipped cream. Arrange cherry halves, about 2 inches apart, in the bottom of a 6-cup round salad mold. Carefully spoon in salad mixture. Chill until firm, at least 2 hours. When ready to serve, unmold onto a chilled serving platter. Serves 8 to 10.

Filled with candies, a paper cone is a special way to spread glad tidings. Roll heavy paper into a cone shape and glue the edges. Once dry, ribbon threaded into holes punched on each side of the cone makes a handle. Left on a neighbor's doorknob or a coworker's chair, it's a sweet December surprise.

Grandma's Wheat Bread

Katie Cooper
Chubbuck, ID

Of course grandmas make the best bread. My grandma created this recipe and it is my favorite for wheat bread. The smell of it baking sends me right back to memories of her home.

2 T. active dry yeast
3 T. gluten
1/2 c. instant mashed
   potato flakes
2 T. powdered milk
3-1/2 c. all-purpose flour

1 t. salt
1-1/2 c. warm water
1/4 c. oil
1/2 c. honey
Garnish: chilled butter

Whisk together yeast, gluten, potato flakes, powdered milk, flour and salt. Heat water to 110 to 115 degrees; stir into flour mixture. Add oil and honey; stir well. Place dough on a lightly floured surface and knead for 10 minutes. Place in a lightly oiled bowl; cover and let rise until double in bulk. Knead again for 5 to 10 minutes. Shape into a loaf and place in a greased 9"x5" loaf pan. Let rise until double. Bake at 350 degrees for 30 minutes, or until golden. Remove pan from oven and spread chilled butter over top of loaf. Makes one loaf.

Craft the sweetest cut-out coasters for friends & family... it's simple using 5-inch squares of wool felt. Use a hole punch to make designs in one square of felt, then top it with fusible webbing cut the same size. Place a second square of felt over the webbing and iron to fuse the pieces together. Trim the edges with pinking or scallop sheers.

Erma Lee's Chicken Soup

Shirley White
Gatesville, TX

*I received this recipe from a dear lady at church. My family still requests
Erma Lee's Chicken Soup at the first sign of colder weather.*

3 14-1/2 oz. cans chicken broth
2/3 c. celery, diced
2/3 c. onion, diced
2/3 c. carrots, peeled and diced
1 c. cooked rice
4 boneless, skinless chicken
   breasts, cooked and chopped

2 10-3/4 oz. cans cream of
   mushroom soup
8-oz. pkg. pasteurized process
   cheese spread, cubed
1 c. shredded Cheddar cheese

Bring broth to a boil in a stockpot over medium heat. Add vegetables;
cook until tender, about 10 minutes. Stir in remaining ingredients;
simmer over low heat until cheeses melt and soup is heated through,
15 minutes. Makes 4 to 6 servings.

Handmade soaps can easily be found at country fairs
and craft shows and are such thoughtful gifts. Keep the
packaging oh-so simple, but special, by placing one or
two blocks of soap on an ironstone dish, add a
soft washcloth and tie up with ribbon.

Vegetable Cheese Chowder

Nancy Mosley
Adairsville, GA

This soup has been our family's traditional Christmas Eve meal for about 25 years. We would come home from our Christmas Eve church service and quickly be warmed by a bowl of steaming chowder served with an assortment of deli sandwiches and a plateful of sweets. This would definitely get us in the Christmas spirit, even in North Georgia when Christmas is usually cold but not white.

4-1/2 c. potatoes, peeled and
    cubed
3/4 c. carrots, peeled and sliced
1/2 c. celery, chopped
1 T. butter
1/2 c. onion
2 cloves garlic, minced

1-1/2 qts. water
3 cubes chicken bouillon
32-oz. pkg. pasteurized process
    cheese spread, cubed
1 to 2 10-3/4 oz. cans cream
    of chicken soup

Place potatoes, carrots and celery in a food processor. Pulse until vegetables are finely chopped. Set aside. Melt butter in a saucepan; add onion and garlic. Sauté until tender. Spoon chopped vegetables and onion mixture into a stockpot. Stir in water and bouillon. Cook over medium heat until vegetables are tender. Add cheese spread and one can of soup; stir to blend. If you prefer a creamier, thicker soup, stir in remaining can of soup. Reduce heat to low and simmer until cheese melts; do not boil. Makes 10 to 12 servings.

Miniature houses look sweet lined up across a mantel. Dress them up for winter with colored lights, tinsel garland, button doorknobs and snowy bottle brush trees.

Wonderful Baked Potato Soup

Shannon Haga
Childress, TX

This is a recipe my mother has always made, and when I got married I began making this for my husband. He LOVES it and makes a request for this soup on a regular basis.

5 baking potatoes, baked and
   cooled
2/3 c. butter
4 to 5 green onions, thinly
   sliced
2/3 c. all-purpose flour
6 c. milk
1-1/2 c. mild shredded Cheddar
   cheese

1 t. salt
1 t. pepper
8-oz. container sour cream
Garnish: shredded Cheddar
   cheese, bacon bits, chopped
   green onion

Cut potatoes in half lengthwise; use a spoon to separate the potato from the potato skins. Discard skins. Melt butter in a saucepan over medium heat. Stir in onions and cook for 2 to 3 minutes. Whisk in flour, stirring constantly until smooth. Stir in milk and increase heat to high. Continue to stir until mixture thickens. Lower heat to medium; add potato, cheese, salt and pepper. Heat through until cheese melts; stir in sour cream. Garnish as desired. Serves 6 to 8.

Give gift cards or movie passes tucked inside easy-to-make pouches. Fold a length of 3-inch wide ribbon in half; stitch the long sides together. Trim the short edges with scallop scissors and slip the gift inside.

Speedy Snow Pea Salad

Linka Chapman
Bakersfield, CA

So speedy to make, I've grabbed a bowl, spoon, measuring cups and stopped at the nearest grocery store on the way to a potluck and whipped this salad up in the car!

16-oz. pkg. frozen peas, thawed
1/2 green onion, chopped
1/2 stalk celery, chopped or
   5-oz. can water chestnuts
   sliced
8-oz. container sour cream

1/2 c. mayonnaise
1/8 c. mayonnaise-type salad
   dressing
3-oz. can bacon bits
8-oz. can cashews

Mix together peas, onion and celery or water chestnuts in a large salad bowl. In a separate bowl, stir together sour cream, mayonnaise and salad dressing; blend well. Spoon sour cream mixture over salad until well coated. At serving time, stir in bacon bits and cashews. Serve immediately. Serves 10.

Nestle votives and tealights on a cake stand sprinkled with rock salt for a sparkling, "snowy" centerpiece.

Make-Ahead Beet & Bean Salad

Karen Larkin
Blue Lake, CA

An absolute family favorite. While it's good any time of year, its red, green and white layers make it especially nice served at Christmastime in a clear glass serving dish. I often combine the drained beet and bean liquids in a cruet or bottle for a wonderful salad dressing.

2 14-oz. cans French-cut green beans, drained and liquid reserved
1-1/2 c. French salad dressing, divided
2 14-oz. cans julienne beets, drained and liquid reserved
1 onion, sliced into thin rings
4 eggs, hard-boiled, peeled and finely chopped
1 c. mayonnaise
1 t. prepared horseradish
salt and pepper to taste
1/2 c. bacon, crisply cooked and crumbled

Place beans in a bowl; stir in 3/4 cup salad dressing. Set aside. In a separate bowl, combine beets and remaining salad dressing. Cover both bowls and refrigerate overnight. In a medium bowl, blend together eggs, mayonnaise, horseradish, salt and pepper. Mix well. In a 13"x9" glass baking pan, layer bean mixture, onion rings and beet mixture. Spoon egg mixture over the top and spread to edges. Sprinkle with crumbled bacon. Cover and chill at least 3 hours before serving. Serves 8 to 12.

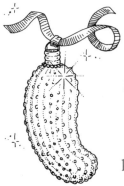

Start a new tradition...hide a glass pickle ornament among the branches of a decorated tree. When it's time to pack away the decorations, whoever finds the pickle gets just one more surprise!

Focaccia Rounds

Jackie Smulski
Lyons, IL

The perfect go-with for any salad.

11-oz. tube refrigerated
   bread sticks
2 t. olive oil

1 t. Italian seasoning
2 T. fresh basil, chopped
2 T. grated Parmesan cheese

Remove bread stick dough from tube; do not unroll. Cut dough into 8 slices. Roll out each slice to a 4-1/2 inch circle. Place circles on a greased baking sheet. Brush dough with oil; sprinkle with seasoning, basil and Parmesan cheese. Bake at 375 degrees for 10 to 15 minutes, until golden. Makes 8 servings.

Tie on your prettiest Christmas apron and invite friends
& family to join you in the kitchen to whip up a favorite
dish. Everyone loves to pitch in, and it's a fun way
to catch up on holiday plans.

Diane's Spinach Salad

Diane Hixon
Niceville, FL

A spin on the usual spinach salad...this one has a chilled,
creamy dressing drizzled on top.

4 c. spinach, torn into bite-size
   pieces
1/2 c. mayonnaise
1/2 c. grated Parmesan cheese
2 T. evaporated milk

1-1/2 t. dill weed
1-1/2 t. dried, chopped onion
1-1/2 t. lemon-pepper
   seasoning

Divide spinach equally among 4 salad bowls; set aside. Whisk
together remaining ingredients, thinning with additional milk, if
desired. Drizzle over spinach. Makes 4 servings.

A scoop of peppermint ice cream added to a frosty glass
of eggnog really dresses it up. To add some fizz,
pour in a splash of chilled ginger ale.

Midwestern Steakhouse Soup

Barbara Cooper
Orion, IL

*If the potatoes haven't thickened the broth as much as you'd like,
simply whisk together 2 tablespoons cornstarch in 1/4 cup cold
water, then stir into the soup and cook a little longer.*

1-1/2 lbs. boneless beef top
   sirloin steak, about 1/2-inch
   thick, sliced into thin strips
2 T. oil
1 sweet onion, sliced
8-oz. pkg. sliced mushrooms
3 14-1/2 oz. cans beef broth

4 c. water
3 potatoes, cut into 1/2-inch
   cubes
2 t. Worcestershire sauce
Garnish: 8-oz. pkg. shredded
   Monterey Jack cheese

In a large soup pot over medium heat, brown steak strips in oil for
5 minutes. Add onion and mushrooms; sauté until tender, about 5 to
10 additional minutes. Add remaining ingredients; simmer over low
heat for 30 to 40 minutes. Transfer to a slow cooker. Cover and cook
on low setting for up to 4 hours. Ladle into bowls and serve garnished
with cheese. Serves 6 to 8.

Soups & stews stay nice and warm when spooned into a
slow cooker that's turned to the low setting. This way,
no matter when family, friends or neighbors arrive
for their visit, the soup will be ready to enjoy.

Slow-Cooker Stroganoff Stew

Jackie Everson
Bangor, WI

My five kids love this...so does everyone else!

1-1/2 lbs. stew beef, cubed
2 T. butter
3 to 4 potatoes, peeled and
    cubed
2 to 3 carrots, peeled and sliced
1/2 c. celery, chopped
1 onion, chopped
1/4 t. dried thyme

1/4 t. pepper
1/8 t. salt
1/2 t. salt-free tomato basil
    garlic seasoning
10-3/4 oz. can cream of
    mushroom soup
1-1/2 c. water
8-oz. container sour cream

Place beef and butter in a large skillet. Cook over medium heat until beef is browned; set aside. Arrange potatoes, carrots, celery and onion in a slow cooker. Sprinkle with seasonings. Stir in beef. Cover and cook on low setting 8 hours. Combine soup, water and sour cream; spoon into slow cooker over beef mixture. Stir to blend. Makes 4 servings.

Create your own spot for a Christmas wish list.
Chalkboard paint is a terrific way to turn practically
any surface into a blackboard. Simply spray an old
cabinet door or even a framed mirror...clever!

Carla's Not Really Chili

Carla Stricklin
Valley Park, MO

When we were expecting a snowstorm, I picked up the essentials at the grocery, thinking I had the ingredients for chili on hand. But, that evening after the snow started in earnest, I realized I was mistaken in that assumption. So, I put this mixture of ingredients into the slow cooker, and it turned out to be quite a hit!

1 lb. lean ground beef, browned and drained
16-oz. can black beans, drained and rinsed
10-oz. can diced tomatoes with green chiles
15-1/4 oz. can corn, drained
2 to 4 T. taco seasoning mix
salt and pepper to taste
1 to 2 c. cocktail vegetable juice to taste
Garnish: sour cream, shredded Cheddar cheese, salsa, chopped green onions

Combine all ingredients except juice and garnish in a slow cooker; stir to blend. Pour in juice until mixture is of desired consistency. Cover and cook at high setting for one to 1-1/2 hours. Reduce to low setting and cook for an additional 30 minutes. Garnish as desired. Makes 4 to 6 servings.

Pile everyone in the car and head to the local cut-your-own tree farm. There's almost always creamy cocoa and snacks to share, and sometimes, even a surprise visit from Santa & Mrs. Claus!

Stone-Ground Corn Rolls

Tina Goodpasture
Meadowview, VA

I manage a country store in Abingdon, Virginia where we have a mill that still is in operation. This is one of my favorite recipes using cornmeal...they are soooo good.

2 c. milk
3/4 c. cornmeal
1/2 c. sugar
1/2 c. shortening
1-1/2 t. salt

1 env. yeast, dissolved in
    1/4 c. warm water
2 eggs, beaten
6 c. all-purpose flour

Combine milk and cornmeal in a large saucepan. Cook over medium heat, stirring frequently, until mixture thickens, about 15 minutes. Remove from heat; add sugar, shortening and salt. Cool slightly. Dissolve yeast in warm water, between 110 and 115 degrees. Add eggs and yeast mixture; slowly stir in flour. Place dough on a lightly floured surface and knead until smooth. Shape dough into 2-inch balls; arrange 2 inches apart on a greased baking sheet. Let rise until double in size. Bake at 375 degrees for 15 minutes. Makes one dozen.

Get together with girlfriends for a Christmas craft night. Ask each friend to bring along an idea and the supplies to share. It's such fun to make gift tags, bath fizzies and ornaments together!

Poblano Corn Chowder

Joshua Logan
Victoria, TX

This is wonderful on a cold winter's night served with toasted Italian or French bread. I usually double the recipe and invite friends over to share it with.

4 c. chicken broth
1 T. sugar
2 14-1/2 oz. cans creamed corn
2 c. potato, peeled and diced
2 to 3 poblano chiles, diced and
    seeds removed
10-oz. pkg. frozen corn, thawed
1 lb. boneless, skinless chicken
    breasts or thighs, cubed
1/2 lb. chorizo pork
    sausage, diced
1 c. whipping cream
1/4 c. fresh cilantro, chopped

In a 6-quart slow cooker, combine all ingredients except cream and cilantro. Cover and cook on low setting for 7 to 8 hours, until chicken is cooked through. Before serving, stir in cream and cilantro; warm through. Serves 8.

Everywhere, everywhere, Christmas tonight!
-Phillips Brooks, Vintage Reader

Chicken Posole

Sandy Roy
Crestwood, KY

This soup reminds me a lot of chicken tortilla soup. It's very easy to make and you can use store-bought rotisserie chicken or leftover Thanksgiving turkey.

2 onions, chopped
1 T. olive oil
8 cloves garlic, minced
1/3 c. tomato paste
3 T. chili powder
1 t. dried oregano
2 t. ground cumin
4 14-1/2 oz. cans chicken broth
15-oz. can diced tomatoes with green chiles
16-oz. pkg. frozen corn, thawed
6-3/4 c. cooked chicken, chopped
salt and pepper to taste
juice of 1 lime
Garnish: chopped avocado, chopped fresh cilantro, thinly sliced radishes, sour cream, sliced green onions, crumbled tortilla chips

In a stockpot, sauté onions in oil until translucent. Add garlic, tomato paste, chili powder, oregano and cumin; stir until thoroughly combined. Add broth. Fill one empty broth can with water; add to stockpot. Stir in tomatoes; bring mixture to a boil. Reduce heat and simmer 30 minutes. Stir in corn, chicken, salt, pepper and lime juice. Cook over medium heat until heated through. Garnish as desired. Makes 8 servings.

Hide lots of waterproof surprises in the snow, then send everyone outside for a wintry scavenger hunt!

Grandmother's Biscuits

Vanessa Scott
Travis AFB, CA

This recipe is my grandmother's and reminds me of time spent with her.

1 env. active dry yeast	5 to 6-1/2 c. all-purpose flour,
1/4 c. water	divided
1/4 c. sugar	4 t. baking powder
1/2 c. oil	1 t. baking soda
2-1/2 c. buttermilk	1 t. salt

In a medium bowl, dissolve yeast in warm water, between 110 to 115 degrees. Add sugar, oil and buttermilk. In a large bowl, sift together 5 cups flour, baking powder, baking soda and salt. Blend in yeast mixture; add more flour if dough is too sticky. Knead dough one minute on a floured board. Roll dough out to 3/4 to one-inch thick. Cut with biscuit cutter. Let rise for 30 minutes. Arrange on ungreased baking sheets. Bake in a 450-degree oven for 15 minutes, until golden. Makes about one dozen.

A regular, quart-size Mason jar filled with peppermint candies, buttons or mini ornaments easily becomes a cheery candle holder. An oyster jar votive holder will sit snugly inside the jar rim, just tuck in the votive.

Garlic Cheddar Biscuit Cups

Kristy Markners
Fort Mill, SC

This is a super easy, fast recipe! I often spoon the batter into giant muffin cups to make 3 oversize biscuits, and then I bake them at 350 degrees for 30 to 35 minutes.

1 c. self-rising flour
1/2 c. shredded Cheddar cheese

3/4 c. fat-free buttermilk
1 t. minced roasted garlic

Combine all ingredients in a medium bowl; mix with a fork. Fill greased or paper-lined muffin cups 3/4 full. Bake at 425 degrees for 17 to 20 minutes, until golden. Makes 6.

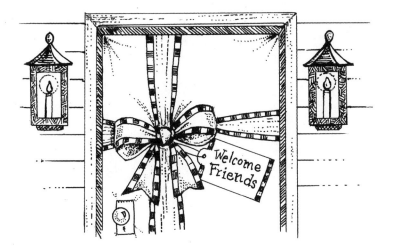

Progressive dinners are a great way to visit with family & friends. Enjoy appetizers at one home, then visit other homes for the salad, main course and dessert.

Roggebrood

Tawnia Hultink
Ontario, Canada

*This is a great Dutch bread recipe. We love slices topped with butter,
and it's also great with a slice of cheese or spread with jam.*

2 c. cracked wheat, rye and flax
   seed hot cereal, uncooked
1 c. whole-wheat flour
1 c. quick-cooking oats,
   uncooked

3/4 c. bran
2 t. baking soda
1 t. salt
1/2 c. dark molasses
2-1/4 c. warm water

In a large bowl, combine cereal, flour, oats, bran, baking soda and
salt. Stir in molasses and water until well blended. Place dough in a
lightly greased 9"x5" loaf pan. Cover pan with aluminum foil and bake
at 325 degrees for 50 minutes. Remove foil and bake 10 minutes
longer. Makes one loaf.

Whip up some snow ice cream...it's creamy and oh-so easy.
Beat one cup heavy cream until soft peaks form, then fold
in 4 cups freshly fallen snow. Add sugar and vanilla to taste.

Tried & True Cranberry Salad

Karen Sylvia
Brighton, CO

*This recipe was made by my grandmother, my mother
and my aunt..now I'm the one making it each holiday.*

16-oz. can whole-berry
  cranberry sauce
8-oz. can crushed pineapple,
  drained

8-oz. container frozen whipped
  topping, thawed
8-oz. container sour cream

Mix all ingredients together in a large bowl. Spoon into a 9"x5" loaf
pan lined with aluminum foil. Freeze for 24 hours. Slice and serve
immediately. Makes about 18 servings.

This year, tuck sparkling beaded necklaces into stockings...
they're surprisingly easy to make! Beads can be found at
craft shops, and thin ribbon or silk beading cord to string
them on come in endless colors. Clasps are attached
to the ribbon at each end with a simple knot.

Mom's Seafood Gumbo

Rhonda Haley
Dade City, FL

This is a recipe my mom handed down to me when I got my first apartment. It is one of my favorites...and so easy!

1 onion, sliced
2 T. butter
16-oz. can stewed tomatoes
1 green pepper, diced
1 clove garlic, diced
1/2 t. salt
1/2 t. cayenne pepper, or to
   taste

1 c. chicken broth
1 lb. uncooked small shrimp,
   peeled and cleaned
6-oz. can crabmeat
1 T. cornstarch
1/4 c. water
10-oz. pkg. frozen sliced okra,
   thawed

Place onion and butter in a microwave-safe 2-quart casserole dish. Microwave on high setting for 4 minutes, or until onions are soft. Stir in remaining ingredients except cornstarch, water and okra. Set aside. In a small bowl, dissolve cornstarch in water. Add to other ingredients; stir well to combine. Stir in okra. Cover dish with wax paper. Microwave on high setting for 25 to 30 minutes, stirring halfway through cooking time. Serves 4.

White ball straight pins can transform a simple red or green pillar candle into a holiday welcome...just push the pins in place to create a snowflake pattern.

Tortellini Soup

Melisa Edge
Yucca Valley, CA

*Try a different variety of stuffed tortellini each time
you prepare this soup...you can't go wrong!*

1 c. onion, chopped
1 clove garlic, minced
1 T. olive oil
15-oz. can crushed tomatoes
9-oz. pkg. cheese-filled
   tortellini, uncooked

14-1/2 oz. can chicken broth
1 T. fresh basil, chopped
9-oz. pkg. baby spinach
salt and pepper to taste

In a saucepan, sauté onion and garlic with oil just until tender. Stir
in tomatoes, tortellini, broth and basil. Simmer over low heat until
tortellini is tender. Add spinach and continue to simmer 5 minutes
longer. Stir in salt and pepper to taste. Serves 8.

Put felt scraps to use by turning them into snowmen
package toppers. Assemble circles with a simple blanket
stitch, just add a little batting to plump them up. Tie
on a felt strip scarf and add a pompom on their caps.

Corn Chip Salad

Lanita Kuhns
Ghent, NY

Everyone will love this salad!

1 head lettuce, chopped
1 lb. bacon, crisply cooked and crumbled
8-oz. pkg. shredded sharp Cheddar cheese
6 eggs, hard-boiled, peeled and chopped
1 c. mayonnaise
2 T. vinegar
1/4 c. milk
1/4 c. sugar
1/4 c. brown sugar, packed
10-oz. pkg. corn chips, crushed

Combine lettuce, bacon, cheese and eggs in a large salad bowl. In a separate bowl, combine remaining ingredients except corn chips; mix together until smooth. Pour over salad, tossing to mix. Top with corn chips just before serving. Makes about 25 servings.

Layered with pretty papers, a plain mailing tag will look terrific tied to any package. Glue on a copy of vintage sheet music trimmed to fit, then layer on paper trees, buttons and a sprinkle of mica snow.

Home
for
Christmas Dinner

Rosemary-Garlic Turkey

Cheri Maxwell
Gulf Breeze, FL

After a trip to a Vermont farm, I was inspired to plant a kitchen garden right outside my back door. With fresh rosemary at my fingertips, this recipe is simple to prepare, but tastes like I was in the kitchen all day.

14-1/2 oz. can chicken broth
1 c. butter, sliced
1/2 c. white wine or chicken
   broth
2 sprigs fresh rosemary
1 lemon, zest removed and fruit
   sliced

2 T. honey
12-lb. turkey, thawed if frozen
1 t. salt
1/2 t. pepper
10 cloves garlic, peeled

Combine broth, butter and wine or broth in a small saucepan; bring to a boil over medium-high heat. Add rosemary and zest; simmer over low for 20 minutes. Stir in honey. Remove from heat; set aside, keeping warm. Pat turkey dry and remove giblets. Sprinkle turkey with salt and pepper. Place turkey breast-side up on a wire rack in a roasting pan. Add lemon slices and garlic to roasting pan. Roast turkey at 350 degrees for about 3 hours, basting with broth mixture every 30 minutes, until a meat thermometer inserted into thigh reads 165 degrees. Transfer to a serving platter; let stand 20 to 30 minutes before carving. Serves 10.

Parsley-buttered potatoes are a delicious side that's ready in no time. Peel, cut and boil potatoes just until tender... toss with butter, salt, pepper and fresh parsley. Yum!

Cranberry-Pecan Stuffing

JoAnn
Gooseberry Patch

This recipe is one of those "must-haves" on our holiday table.

1 c. onion, chopped
1 c. celery, chopped
1/2 c. butter
16-oz. can whole-berry
  cranberry sauce

2 T. chicken bouillon granules
16 slices bread, cubed and dried
1 c. chopped pecans
2 t. poultry seasoning
3 c. water

In a large skillet over medium heat, cook onion and celery in butter until onion is translucent. In a small saucepan over low heat, combine cranberry sauce and bouillon, stirring until bouillon is dissolved. Combine remaining ingredients in a large bowl; add onion and cranberry mixtures. Gently blend. Spoon stuffing into a greased 3-quart casserole dish. Bake, uncovered, at 350 degrees for 30 minutes, or until heated through. Makes 10 to 12 servings.

Snowman pencils are great teacher gifts...for school friends too. Push a pencil eraser into a one-inch foam ball, then glue on the second ball for a head. Brush with glue and dust with white glitter. Add an orange felt nose and marker dots for eyes. Tie on a ribbon scarf and he's done!

Ham with Cumberland Sauce

Geneva Rogers
Gillette, WY

It's the fruity sauce that makes this ham special. Named after the Duke of Cumberland, the sauce was actually created in Germany. All the history aside, you're going to love it!

4 to 5-lb. fully-cooked
   bone-in ham
1/2 c. brown sugar, packed

1 t. dry mustard
1 to 2 t. whole cloves

Using a sharp knife, score ham in diamond shapes. In a medium bowl, combine brown sugar and mustard; spread over ham. Insert a whole clove in center of each diamond. Place ham in a large roaster with a rack. Bake, uncovered, at 325 degrees for 20 to 22 minutes per pound, about one hour and 40 minutes, or until ham is heated through and a meat thermometer reads 140 degrees. Serve with Cumberland Sauce. Serves 8 to 10.

Cumberland Sauce:

1 c. red currant or apple jelly
1/4 c. orange juice
1/4 c. lemon juice

1/4 c. red wine or apple juice
2 T. honey
1 T. cornstarch

Combine ingredients in a medium saucepan. Cook over medium heat until sauce thickens, stirring often. Makes 1-3/4 cups.

Keep a variety of bagged salads in the crisper, and when it's time for dinner, the salad is a breeze to toss together. Tossed with raisins, bacon bits, cheese cubes or croutons, salads can be made to order in no time at all.

Mom's Macaroni & Cheese

Jenny Newman
Goodyear, AZ

My mom has been making this dish since before I was born. As far as I'm concerned, it's the only way to make mac & cheese! I always think of it as a great comfort food, and now I make it for my own family.

8-oz. pkg. elbow macaroni
5-oz. can evaporated milk
1/3 c. water
1 c. milk
3 T. butter

3 T. all-purpose flour
1/2 t. salt
1 T. minced, dried onion
1-1/2 c. shredded sharp
   Cheddar cheese, divided

Cook one cup macaroni according to package instructions; drain. Reserve remaining macaroni for another recipe. Combine evaporated milk, water and milk; set aside. Melt butter in a medium saucepan. Add flour and salt, whisking until flour dissolves. Add onion and evaporated milk mixture, stirring well to avoid lumps. Add cheese. Simmer until cheese melts and sauce is thickened, stirring frequently. Stir in cooked macaroni. Pour into a greased 8"x8" baking pan. Top with remaining cheese and bake, uncovered, at 350 degrees for 30 minutes, or until bubbly and lightly golden. Serves 4 to 6.

Chill December brings the sleet,
Blazing fire, and Christmas treat.
-Sara Coleridge

Pork Scallopini

Nan Wysock
New Port Richey, FL

My family loves this pork and fresh mushroom dish. Using a pork tenderloin makes it very quick & easy to prepare.

2 lbs. pork tenderloin, sliced
   1/2-inch thick
1 c. bread crumbs
1 c. all-purpose flour
1/2 c. butter
1/2 c. oil

16-oz. pkg. sliced mushrooms
1 c. sherry or chicken broth
1 T. dried parsley
1/2 t. salt
cooked rice or noodles

Place pork slices between 2 sheets of wax paper. Gently flatten to 1/4-inch thickness with a rolling pin; set aside. In a large bowl, stir together bread crumbs and flour. Coat pork slices in flour mixture. Add butter and oil to a large saucepan; cook pork over medium-high heat until golden on both sides and cooked through. Remove to a platter and keep warm. In same saucepan, sauté mushrooms until golden; add sherry or broth and parsley. Stir until all browned bits are dissolved. Serve pork slices and sauce over rice or noodles. Serves 4.

Tuck a disposable camera into each stocking so everyone in the family can snap Christmas photos.

Raspberry-Topped Chicken Rolls

Marian Buckley
Fontana, CA

The flavors of blue cheese, bacon and raspberries
make these chicken rolls absolutely the best!

4 boneless, skinless chicken
   breasts
1/2 c. crumbled blue cheese
4 slices bacon, crisply cooked
   and crumbled

1 T. butter, melted
salt and pepper to taste

Place chicken between 2 sheets of wax paper. Using a rolling pin, gently flatten chicken from the center to the outside to a 1/4-inch thickness. Sprinkle chicken with blue cheese and bacon to within 1/2 inch of edges. Roll up, jelly-roll style, starting with a short side; secure with toothpicks. Place in a greased 8"x8" baking pan. Brush with butter; sprinkle with salt and pepper. Bake, uncovered, at 375 degrees for 35 to 40 minutes, until chicken juices run clear. Discard toothpicks; serve with Raspberry Sauce spooned over individual servings. Serves 4.

Raspberry Sauce:

2 c. raspberries
1/4 c. chicken broth
4 t. brown sugar, packed
1 T. balsamic vinegar

1/2 t. garlic, minced
1/4 t. dried oregano
1 T. butter, melted

In a small saucepan, combine all ingredients; bring to a boil over medium heat. Reduce heat; simmer, uncovered, for 5 minutes or until thickened. Press through a sieve or food mill; discard seeds. Stir in butter until mixture is smooth.

Create a dessert table filled with whimsy! Fill milk
bottles with mini marshmallows and slip an oversize
lollipop in each bottle. Finish each off with a
big dotty bow around the bottle necks.

Walnut-Sage Linguine

Angie Whitmore
Farmington, UT

A savory side dish that friends will want the recipe for!

1-1/4 c. half-and-half, divided
3/4 c. chopped walnuts, divided
1/4 c. butter
1 t. dried sage
1/8 t. white pepper

8-oz. pkg. linguine, cooked
1/4 lb. deli ham, cut into
   thin strips
Garnish: fresh parsley

Combine 1/2 cup half-and-half and 1/2 cup walnuts in a blender. Blend until almost smooth. Pour mixture into a medium saucepan. Add remaining half-and-half, butter, sage and pepper. Bring just to boiling. Reduce heat and simmer for 3 to 5 minutes. Pour over hot linguine; add ham and toss gently. Sprinkle each serving with parsley and remaining walnuts. Serves 4.

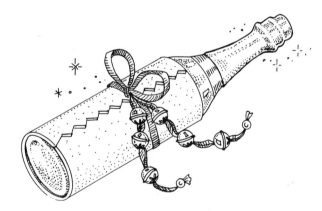

Wrap up a bottle of sparkling cider in style...a thoughtful hostess gift. Use pinking shears to cut a long rectangle from felt. Wrap around the bottle and glue the sides together. Tie it with a ribbon threaded with small jingle bells...perfect!

Mary's Chicken

Julie Otto
Fountainville, PA

My step-mom introduced this chicken dish to me when I was about 10 years old. It's a recipe her neighbor gave to her, hence the name. It has since become a favorite of my husband and many of our family members.

1 c. sour cream
1 T. lemon juice
2 t. Worcestershire sauce
2 cloves garlic, finely chopped
2 t. celery salt
1 t. paprika
1/2 t. pepper

6 boneless, skinless chicken
  breasts
1-1/2 c. Italian-flavored dry
  bread crumbs
1/4 c. butter
1/4 c. shortening

Combine sour cream, lemon juice, Worcestershire sauce, garlic, celery salt, paprika and pepper in a large bowl. Add chicken and coat well. Refrigerate overnight. Remove chicken from mixture and roll in bread crumbs. Arrange in a single layer in a lightly greased 15"x10" jelly-roll pan. In a saucepan, melt butter and shortening; spoon half over chicken. Bake, uncovered, at 350 degrees for 45 minutes. Spoon remaining butter mixture over chicken and bake for 10 to 15 minutes longer, until golden and juices run clear. Serves 4 to 6.

Retro-style ornaments that take just minutes to craft! Give a plain die-cut tree a spritz of spray adhesive and a layer of polka dot paper trimmed to fit. Add another light spray of adhesive and a sprinkling of mica snow for shimmer.

Aunt Helen's Roast

Lynn Williams
Muncie, IN

*There is nothing, absolutely nothing, like walking in the door
to the aroma of this roast cooking. I love it with a side of
honey-glazed carrots and parsley-buttered potatoes.*

3-lb. boneless beef sirloin
  tip roast
1-1/4 c. water, divided
8-oz. can sliced mushrooms,
  drained

1.35-oz. pkg. onion soup mix
3 T. cornstarch

Line a shallow roasting pan with aluminum foil. Place roast on foil.
Pour one cup water and mushrooms over roast; sprinkle with soup
mix. Wrap foil around roast; seal tightly. Bake at 350 degrees for
2-1/2 to 3 hours, or until meat reaches desired doneness: 145 degrees
for medium-rare, 160 degrees for medium or 170 degrees for well
done. Remove roast to a serving platter and cover to keep warm.
Pour pan drippings and mushrooms into a saucepan. Whisk together
cornstarch and remaining water until smooth; gradually stir into
drippings. Bring to a boil; cook and stir until thickened. Serve sauce
with sliced beef. Serves 8 to 10.

A scoop of peppermint ice cream is yummy sandwiched
between two sugar cookies...dessert in no time!

Snowy White Mashed Potatoes

Kristin Santangelo-Winterhoff
Rochester, NY

I first tried these potatoes at my aunt's house during Christmas, and decided they were the best mashed potatoes I'd ever had! They are so rich and creamy, you can't stop at one helping.

5 lbs. potatoes, peeled, cooked
   and mashed
1 c. sour cream
8-oz. pkg. cream cheese,
   softened
1/4 c. butter, melted

1/4 t. granulated garlic
1 t. salt
1 t. pepper
1/8 t. dried parsley
3 T. butter, sliced
1/8 t. paprika

In a medium bowl, beat together all ingredients except butter and paprika. Spoon potatoes into a greased 2-quart casserole dish. Dot potatoes with butter. Sprinkle paprika over potatoes. Bake, covered, at 350 degrees for 25 minutes. Serves 8 to 10.

Beeswax candles have such a sweet fragrance...
wrap up a bundle and tie with a length of wide
rick rack for a gift from the heart.

Cranberry-Apple Bake

Macie Dilling
Raleigh, NC

Several years ago a good friend shared this side dish with me.
Its sweet-tart flavor is perfect alongside savory turkey and dressing.

3 c. apples, cored, peeled and
   chopped
2 c. cranberries
1/2 c. plus 2 T. all-purpose flour,
   divided
1 c. sugar

3 1-5/8 oz. pkgs. instant
   cinnamon and spice oats
3/4 c. chopped pecans
1/2 c. brown sugar, packed
1/2 c. butter, melted

In a large bowl, combine apples, cranberries and 2 tablespoons flour. Toss to coat fruit. Add sugar, mixing well. Place in a lightly greased 2-quart casserole dish. In a medium bowl, combine oats, pecans, remaining flour and brown sugar. Blend in butter. Spoon oat mixture over fruit. Bake, uncovered, at 350 degrees for 45 minutes. Makes 12 servings.

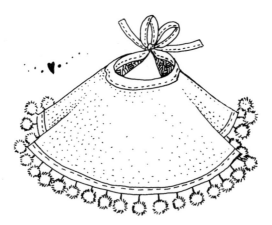

For a quick-as-a-wink tree skirt, stitch a white pompom garland across a length of red fleece...easy!

Caramelized Sweet Potatoes

Lorraine Langis
British Columbia, Canada

I wasn't a big sweet potato fan before my stepmother-in-law shared this recipe with me, but let me tell you, they are delicious! Even my kids love them. One of the best things about this recipe is it's ready to hit the table in less than 30 minutes, and with very little prep work.

4 t. butter
2 red or white onions, cut into
   3/4-inch pieces
2 sweet potatoes, peeled and
   cut into 1/2-inch cubes

1/4 c. water
2 T. brown sugar, packed
3/4 t. fresh rosemary, minced

Melt butter in a large skillet over medium-high heat. Stir in onions and cook for 3 to 4 minutes, stirring frequently. Add sweet potatoes and water; reduce heat to medium. Cover and cook for 10 to 12 minutes, or until sweet potatoes are nearly tender, stirring occasionally. Add brown sugar and rosemary. Uncover and cook, stirring gently, over medium-low heat for 4 to 5 minutes, or until onions and sweet potatoes are glazed. Makes 4 servings.

Candy cane-style napkin rings that are so simple...twist together red and white pipe cleaners and slip napkins inside.

Chicken & Cornbread Dressing

Lorrie Smith
Drummonds, TN

*This dressing has been served at every Thanksgiving
and Christmas dinner in my family for generations.
Nobody makes it like my mother...hers is the best!*

8-1/2 oz. pkg. cornbread mix,
   prepared and crumbled
3-lb. chicken
2 14-1/2 oz. cans chicken broth
5 to 6 stalks celery, chopped
1 onion, chopped

1 T. oil
2 eggs, hard-boiled, peeled and
   finely chopped
1 T. dried sage
salt and pepper to taste
3 to 4 slices day-old bread, torn

Place chicken and broth in a 5-quart Dutch oven. If necessary, add enough water to cover chicken. Simmer for one hour, or until chicken is tender and juices run clear. Remove chicken from broth and set aside to cool. In a medium saucepan, sauté celery and onion in oil until onion is translucent. Add celery mixture, eggs and seasonings to broth. Simmer for 15 minutes. Remove and discard chicken bones. Return chicken to broth. Add bread and cornbread to broth; consistency will be thick. Spoon into a greased 14"x11" baking pan. Bake, uncovered, at 375 degrees for 45 minutes, or until top is firm and lightly golden. Serves 8.

A tiered cake stand is just right for holding a variety of breads to serve with dinner. Fill the tiers with savory garlic knots, slices of marble rye, crescent rolls and bread sticks.

Ham Tetrazzini

Cheri Emery
Quincy, IL

Quick & easy, and oh-so delicious!

10-3/4 oz. can cream of
   mushroom soup
1/2 c. milk
1-1/2 c. shredded Cheddar
   cheese

1 lb. cooked ham, diced
6-oz. pkg. spaghetti, cooked
salt and pepper to taste

Combine soup, milk and cheese in a large skillet over medium heat. Cook and stir until cheese melts. Stir in ham, spaghetti, salt and pepper; heat through. Serves 4.

Welcome family & friends home with the scent of cinnamon. Place water and a sprinkling of cinnamon and pumpkin pie spice in a kettle and set over low heat to simmer.

Lemon-Bacon Brussels Sprouts

Laura Witham
Anchorage, AK

Very few members of my family have a weakness for veggies, especially Brussels sprouts. So after experimenting with flavors that I knew everyone liked, I came up with this recipe as a last-ditch effort to get my family to eat some veggies before they devoured the pumpkin pie. And guess what? It worked!

12-oz. pkg. bacon, diced, crisply
   cooked and drippings
   reserved
4 cloves garlic, minced
4 shallots, finely diced
1/4 c. dry white wine or chicken
   broth

2 lbs. frozen Brussels sprouts,
   thawed
1 T. Italian seasoning
salt and pepper to taste
2 c. chicken broth, divided
zest and juice of one lemon

In a large skillet over medium-high heat, sauté garlic and shallots in 2 tablespoons reserved bacon drippings. When shallots are tender, add wine or 1/4 cup broth. Bring to a boil over high heat; scrape down sides of pan with a spoon to loosen brown bits. Once liquid is reduced, remove shallot mixture and remaining liquid to a bowl; set aside. Add Brussels sprouts to skillet and cook on medium-high heat until they begin to turn golden. Stir in Italian seasoning, salt and pepper. Begin gradually adding broth 1/2 cup at a time. Wait for broth to be cooked down before adding the next 1/2 cup. Stir gently. When the last of the broth has been added and cooked down, reduce heat to medium-low and return bacon, garlic and shallots to the skillet. Stir slowly, adding lemon zest and juice. Serve immediately. Serves 6.

Need a tablecloth fast? Simply toss a quilt on the table!

The Juiciest Turkey Breast

Aimee Warner
Delaware, OH

This recipe is so simple!

5-1/2 lb. turkey breast, thawed
4 t. Italian seasoning
2 t. seasoned salt
3/4 t. pepper
1 c. water

Place turkey breast on a rack in a shallow roasting pan. Sprinkle with seasonings and tent with aluminum foil. Bake at 350 degrees for one hour. Remove foil and add water to pan. Continue baking for an additional 1 to 1-1/2 hours, or until internal temperature reaches 170 degrees. Baste occasionally with pan juices. Remove from oven and let stand 15 minutes before carving. Serves 8.

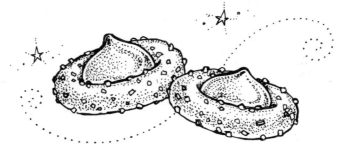

For the quickest bite-size treats, arrange round pretzels on a baking sheet; place a chocolate drop in the center of each. Bake one to 2 minutes in a 350-degree oven, remove from oven and place a candy-coated chocolate in the center of each. Refrigerate until chilled. Yummy!

Nutted Wild Rice

Judy Young
Shaker Heights, OH

*These flavor combinations in this recipe match well with meat
or chicken. Don't pass this one up until you try it!*

1 c. wild rice, uncooked
5-1/2 c. chicken broth
1 c. pecan halves
1 c. golden raisins
zest of 1 orange

1/4 c. fresh mint, chopped
4 green onions, sliced
1/4 c. olive oil
1/3 c. orange juice
1/8 t. pepper

Place rice and broth in a medium saucepan. Bring to a boil; reduce
heat and simmer, covered, 40 minutes. Drain liquid and spoon rice
into a large bowl. When rice has cooled, add pecans, raisins, orange
zest, mint and onions, tossing well. Stir in oil and orange juice;
sprinkle with pepper. Serve at room temperature. Makes 6 servings.

For a new spin on a traditional Advent calendar,
tuck notes, wrapped candies and games into a
stocking garland...a great way to count down
the days until Santa's visit!

Tangy Beef Dijon

Tiffany Brinkley
Broomfield, CO

This dish marinates overnight, freeing me up to spend time with family & friends during their holiday visits.

1 T. Dijon mustard	1/4 t. dried tarragon
1-1/2 t. prepared horseradish	1/4 t. pepper
1/4 t. dried basil	2 8-oz. beef tenderloin steaks
1/4 t. dried thyme	salt to taste

In a small bowl, stir together mustard, horseradish, basil, thyme, tarragon and pepper. Spread mixture evenly over both sides of steaks. Wrap each steak individually with plastic wrap; refrigerate overnight. When ready to bake, spray a glass 9"x9" baking pan with non-stick vegetable spray. Unwrap steaks and sprinkle with salt. Arrange steaks in baking pan and bake at 400 degrees to desired doneness, 30 minutes for medium-rare, 60 minutes for well-done. Serves 2.

Jams, jellies and layered mixes are tasty gifts from the kitchen. Top off jars in clever ways with mini wreaths, little ornaments, chipboard initials or felted snowflakes.

Spanish Chicken

Erin Geddie
Fort Worth, TX

Toss the ingredients into the slow cooker, turn it on and forget about it!

4 boneless, skinless chicken
   breasts
salt and pepper to taste
1 t. paprika
6-oz. can tomato paste

12-oz. can beer or non-alcoholic
   beer
Optional: 7-oz. jar green olives
   with pimentos
cooked rice

Sprinkle both sides of chicken breasts with salt, pepper and paprika. Arrange chicken in a slow cooker. In a small bowl, whisk together tomato paste and beer; pour over chicken. Add olives with liquid to slow cooker, if using. Cover and cook on low setting for 8 to 10 hours. Serve over cooked rice. Serves 4.

Tie dog bones and toys to a greenery wreath
using raffia...the perfect pooch present!

Spinach-Rice Bake

Mary Ellen Farrell
Ludlow, KY

This has been at every family Thanksgiving and Christmas! It is my brother's favorite recipe. My mom and aunt have even made additional batches for him to take back to law school after the holidays.

10-oz. pkg. frozen chopped
   spinach, cooked and drained
1 c. cooked rice
1 c. shredded sharp Cheddar
   cheese
2 eggs, beaten

3 T. margarine, softened
2 T. onion, chopped
1 t. salt
1/3 c. milk
1/2 t. Worcestershire sauce

Combine spinach, rice, cheese, eggs, margarine, onion and salt in a large bowl. Blend in milk to desired consistency and Worcestershire sauce. Spoon mixture into a greased 9"x9" baking pan. Bake, covered for 30 minutes at 350 degrees. Uncover and bake for an additional 30 minutes. Serves 6.

White acrylic paint is great for adding white candy cane stripes to a red enamelware pail. Filled with little surprises or sweet treats, it's an oh-so cheery gift!

Cranberry Cider Chicken

Sandy McGary Chandler
Champaign, IL

This recipe holds special memories for me. My family loves it and we always prepare it for special occasions and for holidays.

4 to 6 boneless, skinless
   chicken breasts
2 c. Cranberry Cider
1 T. whole cloves
4 4-inch cinnamon sticks

1 c. sweetened dried cranberries
2 apples, cored, peeled and
   quartered
1 orange, peeled and sectioned
Optional: orange slices

Arrange chicken in a lightly greased roasting pan; pour cider over all. Place cloves and cinnamon sticks in a square of cheesecloth; tie closed with kitchen string. Add to roasting pan with dried cranberries. Bake, uncovered, at 350 degrees for 2 hours, or until juices run clear when chicken is pierced. Add apples and orange to roasting pan; return to oven until orange is warm, about 5 minutes. Garnish servings with slices of orange, if desired. Serves 4 to 6.

Cranberry Cider:

1.2-oz. pkg. mulling spice mix   4 c. cranberry juice cocktail

Combine spice mix and juice in a medium saucepan; bring to steaming over medium heat. Stir well. Makes 4 cups.

Celebrate Christmas
Texas-style...set out
cowboy boots in front
of the fireplace instead
of hanging stockings!

Brown Sugar-Applesauce Bake

Karen Skocik
Palos Heights, IL

The holidays just wouldn't be the same without this dish.
When served, the recipe always goes home with someone.

25-oz. jar applesauce	1 c. biscuit baking mix
1/2 c. brown sugar, packed	1/2 c. sugar
1 t. cinnamon	1/4 c. margarine, softened

In a medium bowl, combine applesauce, brown sugar and cinnamon. Spoon into a 1-1/2 quart casserole dish sprayed with non-stick vegetable spray. In a small bowl, blend together baking mix, sugar and margarine until crumbly; sprinkle over applesauce mixture. Bake, uncovered, for one hour at 350 degrees. Stir before serving. Serves 8 to 10.

Filled with cookies or candies, gift cards or movie passes,
a retro lunchbox makes a great gift box!

Apricot-Glazed Chicken Breasts

Sharon Demers
Dolores, CO

If there are any leftovers, make the next day's lunch in a snap. I love to cut the chicken in strips and serve over a bed of mixed greens with glazed pecans, crumbled gorgonzola cheese and pear slices, then drizzle with a balsamic vinaigrette.

4 boneless, skinless chicken
   breasts
salt and pepper to taste

12-oz. jar apricot jam
2 T. honey
2 T. Dijon mustard

Arrange chicken in a 13"x9" glass baking pan sprayed with non-stick vegetable spray. Sprinkle with salt and pepper; set aside. Bring jam, honey and mustard to a boil in a small saucepan over medium heat. Reduce heat to low; simmer until mixture is thickened and reduced by half. Spoon apricot sauce over chicken breasts, coating evenly. Bake at 425 degrees, for 30 to 40 minutes, basting with sauce every 10 minutes. Continue to bake until juices run clear when chicken is pierced with a fork. Serves 4.

Christmas bazaars are so much fun...jot down the dates on your calendar and invite girlfriends to come along. These get-togethers are filled with one-of-a-kind handmade items and scrumptious homebaked goodies that are just too good to pass up!

Chicken Kiev

Grecia Williams
Scottsville, KY

My daughters always request this dish
when they come home from college.

1-1/2 c. dry bread crumbs
1/2 c. shredded Parmesan
  cheese
1 t. dried basil
1 t. dried oregano
1/2 t. garlic salt
1/2 t. salt

1-1/2 lbs. chicken tenders
2/3 c. butter, melted
1/4 c. white wine or chicken
  broth
1/4 c. green onion, chopped
1/4 c. dried parsley

Combine bread crumbs, cheese and seasonings in a large bowl.
Dip chicken in melted butter; reserve butter. Roll chicken in crumb
mixture. Arrange chicken in a greased 13"x9" baking pan. Bake,
covered, at 375 degrees for 30 to 40 minutes, until chicken is tender.
To a small saucepan, add wine or broth, onion, parsley and reserved
butter; heat until warm. Spoon over chicken and continue to bake,
covered, for 5 to 7 minutes. Serves 6 to 8.

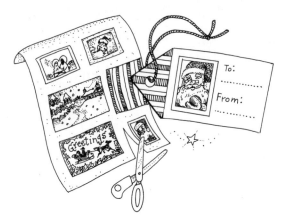

Scan family photos, old postcards or wrapping paper on a
computer and turn them into Christmas mailing labels...
just add the "To" and "From" addresses.

Nippy Carrots

Faye Mayberry
Saint David, AZ

I can't resist sharing a recipe from my grandmother. I wasn't too sure about this dish when I saw the horseradish, but I made it and it really is flavorful. The sugar balances out the tanginess of the horseradish and I love it!

3 c. carrots, peeled and sliced
1 t. prepared horseradish
1 T. sugar

2 T. butter
salt to taste
1/8 t. pepper

In a medium saucepan, cook carrots in a small amount of salted water until tender; drain. Add remaining ingredients and stir gently over low heat for about 5 minutes, until glazed. Serves 4.

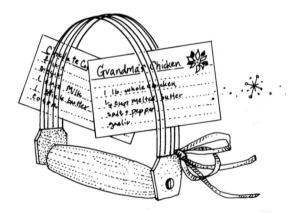

Delight your family with a few of
Grandma's best recipes...tuck recipe
cards into a vintage pastry blender.

Cheery Cherry Punch, page 204

Maple Ham & Egg Cups, page 37

Apricot Oat Breakfast, page 31

Festive Brunch Frittata,
page 40

White Chocolate Party Mix, page 69

Feta Cheese Ball, page 63

Bacon Quesadillas, page 57

Midwestern Steakhouse Soup, page 90

Easy Beef Burgundy, page 144

Green Bean Delight, page 133

Cocoa & Coffee Sheet Cake, page 183

Poblano Corn Chowder, page 94

Grandma's Pecan Balls, page 209

Sun-Dried Tomato Toasties, page 52

Savory Cornish Hens, page 132

Dianna's Best Tiramisu,
page 173

Taco Lasagna, page 149

Snowballs, page 187

Honeyed Fruit Juice, page 51

Perfect Rolls, page 75

Cran-Orange Pork Medallions, page 129

Christmas Peppermint &
Chocolate Meringes, page 198

Cran-Orange Pork Medallions

Vickie
Gooseberry Patch

Ready in just 30 minutes...what a timesaver!

1 to 1-1/2 lb. pork tenderloin,
   cut into 1-inch slices
1/2 t. salt
1/2 t. garlic powder
1/2 t. coriander
1/4 t. pepper
2 T. olive oil

1 medium red onion, chopped
1/2 c. orange marmalade
1/4 c. orange juice
1/4 c. sweetened dried
   cranberries
2 T. balsamic vinegar

Place pork between two pieces of wax paper. Using a rolling pin, flatten to 1/4-inch thickness. Combine seasonings; sprinkle over both sides of pork. In a large skillet, sauté pork in oil for 3 minutes on each side, or until juices run clear. Remove and keep warm. In same skillet, sauté onion in pan juices for 5 minutes, or until tender. Stir in marmalade, orange juice, cranberries and vinegar. Bring to a boil. Reduce heat; return pork to skillet. Simmer, uncovered, for 5 minutes, or until sauce is thickened. Makes 4 servings.

Make some quick & easy fire starters for a frosty winter day. Bundle newspaper into 6-inch squares and secure with natural twine. Tuck under firewood and light with a match...so simple.

Southern-Style Cabbage

Patricia Cherry
Rock Hill, SC

*Each year at Christmas, my nephew, Ray, always asks for my
cabbage casserole. I can't seem to make enough of them!*

1 head cabbage, quartered,
  sliced and divided
1 onion, sliced and divided
2 10-3/4 oz. cans cream of
  mushroom soup

8-oz. pkg. shredded Cheddar
  cheese

Spray a 13"x9" baking pan with non-stick vegetable spray. Place half
the cabbage into pan; top with half the onion. Spread soup over onion;
repeat layers. Sprinkle with cheese. Bake, covered, at 350 degrees
for 40 to 45 minutes, or until cabbage is tender. Serves 6 to 8.

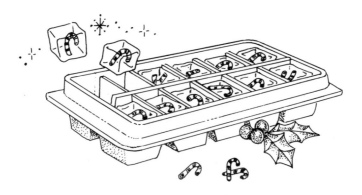

When it's time to make ice cubes, freeze mini candy canes
along with the water...they look very merry floating
in a punch bowl or glass of orange juice!

Shrimp Étouffée

Anne Hansel
Houston, TX

This wonderful Creole dish is very popular in New Orleans.

1 onion, chopped
1 stalk celery, chopped
1/2 c. margarine
1 green pepper, chopped
1/2 t. salt
1/2 t. pepper
1 t. cayenne pepper

10-3/4 oz. can cream of
   mushroom soup
8-oz. can tomato sauce
1 lb. uncooked medium shrimp,
   peeled and cleaned
cooked rice

In a large saucepan over medium heat, sauté onion and celery in margarine for about 10 minutes. Add green pepper and seasonings; cook 10 minutes more. Stir in soup, sauce and shrimp. Cook for 30 minutes over medium-low heat. Serve over rice. Serves 4.

Worn retro fabrics, quilt squares and flour sacks are found for a song at flea markets...use the best parts and stitch up one-of-a-kind cuffs for Christmas stockings.

Savory Cornish Hens

Kendall Hale
Lynn, MA

My roomy 6-quart slow cooker is perfect for this recipe.

4 20-oz. Cornish game hens,
  thawed
2 T. oil
4 redskin potatoes, sliced
  1/8-inch thick

4 slices bacon, cut into 1-inch
  pieces
lemon-pepper seasoning and
  garlic powder to taste
Garnish: fresh parsley, minced

Brown hens in oil in a large skillet over medium heat. Arrange potato slices in a slow cooker; top with hens and bacon. Sprinkle with lemon-pepper and garlic powder. Cover and cook on low setting for 6 to 8 hours, or until chicken juices run clear and potatoes are tender. Garnish with parsley. Serves 4.

Aprons are practical, but also adorable! Look for the 1950s style with poinsettias, snowmen and Santa Claus... perfect gifts for girlfriends who love to cook.

Green Bean Delight

Beth Bennett
Stratham, NH

Memories of Christmas dinner with family always
included this side dish.

4 16-oz. cans green beans, drained
1-oz. pkg. ranch salad dressing mix
2 10-3/4 oz. cans cream of
   mushroom soup
1/4 c. milk

8-oz. pkg. shredded Colby
   Jack cheese
1 c. sliced almonds or cashews
2.8-oz. can French fried onions

Spread green beans in a lightly greased 13"x9" baking pan; set aside.
Combine salad dressing mix, soup and milk in a bowl; drizzle over beans.
Sprinkle with cheese, nuts and onions. Bake, uncovered, at 350 degrees
for 25 minutes. Serves 8 to 10.

Keep the holidays organized by using roomy pantry jars
to hold everything from ribbons and bows to wish lists
and recipes. Cut wallpaper for labels and secure
to the jars with double-sided tape.

Grandmother's Broccoli Casserole
Christine Ceprish
Tionesta, PA

*Handed down from my grandmother, this casserole is sure
to please during the holidays, or any time.*

20-oz. pkg. frozen chopped
  broccoli, thawed
8-oz. pkg. shredded mozzarella
  cheese
10-3/4 oz. can cream of
  mushroom soup

3 c. croutons
1/2 c. butter, melted
16-oz. pkg. ground pork
  sausage, browned

In a large bowl, combine broccoli, cheese, soup, croutons and butter.
Blend in sausage. Spoon mixture into a greased 13"x9" baking pan.
Bake, uncovered, at 350 degrees for 45 minutes. Makes 8 servings.

Take dessert outside 'round a wintry campfire...
roasted apples rolled in cinnamon-sugar are delicious!

Shoepeg Corn Casserole

Ginger Robertson
Belden, MS

A traditional dish I make every Thanksgiving and Christmas.

10-3/4 oz. can cream of
  celery soup
1 pt. sour cream
1/2 c. butter, melted
1 sleeve round buttery crackers,
  crushed
2 15-oz. cans shoepeg corn,
  drained and divided

13-oz. can French-cut green
  beans, drained
1/2 c. onion, chopped
5-oz. can sliced water chestnuts,
  drained
1 c. shredded sharp Cheddar
  cheese

Combine soup and sour cream in a small bowl; set aside. In a separate bowl, blend together butter and cracker crumbs; set aside. In a greased 13"x9" baking pan, layer as follows: one can corn, green beans, remaining corn, onion, water chestnuts, cheese and soup mixture. Top with crumb mixture. Bake, covered, at 350 degrees for 25 minutes. Remove cover and bake an additional 20 minutes. Serves 10.

When boxing up gifts to mail, try something new.
Wrapped candies, crumpled sheet music and
wrapping paper are all terrific ideas for filler...
and much more fun than foam peanuts!

Fancy Pants Chicken

Cathy Forbes
Hutchinson, KS

I served this simple, but elegant chicken dish over almond rice pilaf for my daughter and her friends for their Winter Formal dinner. Several of the other moms and I got together to prepare dinner for the girls and their dates. Our home was decorated to suit the winter theme and we brought out the china and silver. The moms served as waiters...we had a ball!

12 chicken breast tenders
2 T. olive oil
1/3 c. teriyaki marinade sauce
1/2 c. ranch salad dressing

6 to 8 slices bacon, cooked
   and crumbled
1 c. shredded Colby Jack cheese

In a large skillet over medium heat, lightly brown chicken in oil. Remove chicken and place in a lightly greased 11"x7" baking pan. Brush both sides of chicken generously with teriyaki sauce. Top with salad dressing, crumbled bacon and cheese. Bake, uncovered, at 350 degrees until chicken juices run clear, about 10 to 15 minutes. Serves 6.

Keep all your hot cocoa must-haves together using enamelware cake pans or vintage serving trays. Marshmallows, whipped cream, shakers of cinnamon or cocoa and peppermint sticks will be right at your fingertips.

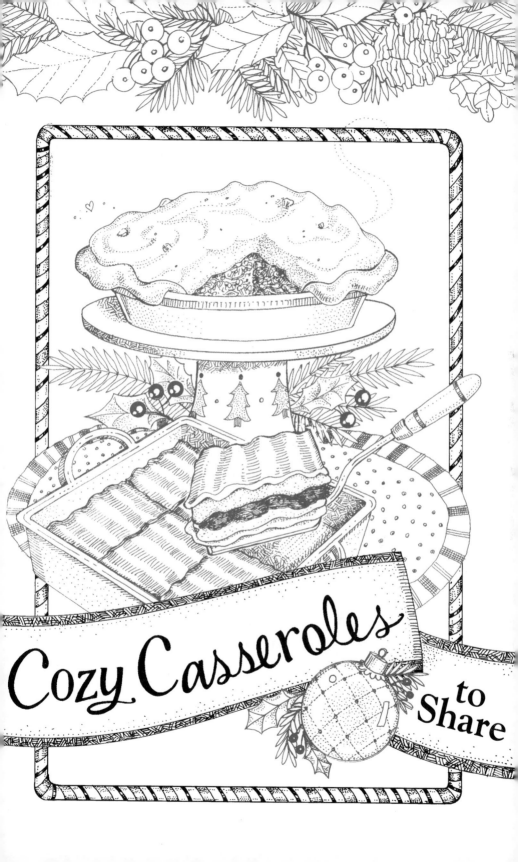

Cozy Casseroles to Share

Florence's Meatball Casserole

Kim Watkins
Wagoner, OK

My grandmother, Florence Reed, used to make this dish every time I would visit. It is my favorite comfort food, and she had a special spoon that she would always use for serving. When she passed away I received the spoon. Now I serve Grandmother's meatball casserole with that same special serving spoon.

1 lb. lean ground beef
1 egg, beaten
1 onion, diced
1/2 green pepper, diced
salt and pepper to taste
2 10-3/4 oz. cans cream of
   mushroom soup

1-1/4 c. water
16-oz. container sour cream
7-oz. pkg. elbow macaroni,
   cooked
15-1/4 oz. can peas, drained

Mix ground beef, egg, onion and green pepper in a medium bowl. Add salt and pepper to taste. Shape mixture into small meatballs and place in a skillet. Brown on all sides. Drain and remove from skillet. In a large bowl, blend together soup, water, sour cream and macaroni. Add peas and meatballs; stir well. Place in a lightly greased 2-quart casserole dish. Bake, covered, at 350 degrees for 30 to 40 minutes. Serves 6 to 8.

Make it a homespun holiday...
arrange evergreen branches
in a sap bucket and decorate
with vintage glass ornaments.

Chicken Parmigiana Casserole

Nancy Girard
Chesapeake, VA

This is an easy way to get all the flavor of chicken parmigiana without all the fuss!

1 c. Italian-flavored dry bread crumbs
1/3 c. grated Parmesan cheese
1 lb. boneless, skinless chicken breasts, cut into bite-size pieces
1 T. butter
1 T. olive oil
16-oz. pkg. penne pasta, cooked
26-oz. jar marinara sauce, divided
1 c. shredded mozzarella cheese, divided

Combine bread crumbs and Parmesan cheese in a large plastic zipping bag. Place chicken in bag and shake to coat. In a medium saucepan, heat butter and oil together over medium heat. Add chicken to saucepan and brown on all sides. In an ungreased 13"x9" baking pan, layer pasta, half of sauce, half of cheese and chicken. Top with remaining sauce and cheese. Bake, covered at 350 degrees for 30 minutes, or until heated through and cheese is melted and bubbly. Makes 6 servings.

Take the no-fuss approach when putting names on stockings. Write names on mailing tags, then trim the edges with decorative-edged scissors and tie on.

Pizza Noodle Bake

Linda Diepholz
Lakeville, MN

I first made this recipe for our family luncheon after my son's baptism. My son is now in college, and I'm still serving this...it's always a big hit.

1 lb. ground beef
1 c. onion, chopped
8-oz. pkg. wide egg noodles, cooked
10-1/2 oz. can pizza sauce
10-3/4 oz. can Cheddar cheese soup

8-oz. can sliced mushrooms, drained
2-1/2 c. shredded mozzarella cheese

Brown ground beef with onion in a medium skillet; drain. Stir in noodles, sauce, soup and mushrooms. Spoon mixture into a greased 13"x9" baking pan. Bake, covered at 350 degrees for 35 to 45 minutes, or until heated through. Sprinkle with mozzarella cheese and bake 5 minutes longer, or until cheese is melted. Serves 6 to 8.

Mix old and new Santa decorations for a quick centerpiece...just arrange them in the center of a cedar wreath. Oh-so easy!

Pepperoni Lasagna

Jackie Heeter
Bartlesville, OK

This is the first dish that my husband ever cooked for me. We were in our first year of marriage, and when I worked evenings, I came home to this for dinner. Sixteen years later, we still make this delicious lasagna, and my family loves it!

9 lasagna noodles, cooked
3-1/2 oz. pkg. sliced pepperoni
2-2/3 c. pizza sauce

3 to 4 c. shredded mozzarella
   cheese

Coat the inside of a 13"x9" baking pan with non-stick vegetable spray. Layer 3 noodles in bottom of pan and spread on a layer of sauce. Continue to layer with pepperoni, mozzarella, noodles and sauce. Repeat layers 2 times. Cover with aluminum foil and bake at 350 degrees for 30 minutes. Remove foil and continue to bake another 10 to 15 minutes, or until golden. Makes 12 servings.

Personalized snow globes make the sweetest place markers. Plastic snow globes with an opening on the bottom can easily be found at craft stores...simply insert a photo into the opening.

Chicken & Stuffing Rolls

Tulsa-Leigh Carlson
Sioux Falls, SD

Two of my husband's dinnertime favorites are stuffing and gravy.
Mix them together with a few other ingredients, and ta-da...
my husband's new favorite dinner!

6-oz. pkg. chicken-flavored
    stuffing mix, prepared
2 12-oz. jars chicken gravy,
    divided
2 c. cooked chicken, sliced into
    strips

14-1/2 oz. can green beans,
    drained
6 12-inch flour tortillas
4-oz. can sliced mushrooms,
    drained
lemon-pepper seasoning to taste

Pour one jar of gravy into a lightly greased 13"x9" baking pan. Set
aside. Divide prepared stuffing, chicken and green beans equally
between 6 tortillas. Roll tortillas and place seam-side down in baking
dish. Top with remaining jar of gravy and mushrooms, sprinkle with
seasoning. Cover and bake at 350 degrees for 30 to 40 minutes. Let
stand 5 minutes before serving. Serves 6.

A little washable poster paint and a brush is all that's
needed to write cheery holiday greetings on mirrors
or windows. And with a little soapy water,
it will easily wash off after the holidays.

Cornbread Casserole

Kimberly Lawson
Rosharon, TX

This casserole recipe, passed down from my aunt to me, is always a favorite dinnertime dish. Every time I prepare it, I think of her.

1 lb. ground beef
1-1/4 oz. pkg. taco seasoning
  mix
1/4 c. water
16-oz. pkg. jalapeño cornbread
  mix

1 egg, beaten
1/2 c. milk
12-oz. pkg. American cheese
  slices
2 14-3/4 oz. cans creamed corn

Brown ground beef in a large skillet over medium heat. Drain; add taco seasoning and water. Prepare cornbread mix using egg and milk. Bake according to package directions. When cool, crumble cornbread and place half in a lightly greased 13"x9" baking pan. Layer half of each, ground beef mixture, cheese and corn over cornbread; repeat with remaining ingredients. Top with reserved cornbread. Bake, uncovered, at 350 degrees for 35 to 45 minutes, or until top is golden. Serves 6 to 8.

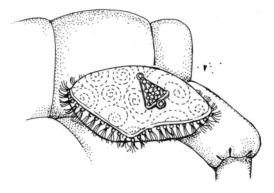

Vintage shops turn up the prettiest treasures. A glittery brooch pinned to the center of a bow will really make a special gift sparkle.

Easy Beef Burgundy

Laurie Aitken
Walden, NY

A simple-to-make version of this classic dish...great for company.

2 lbs. stew beef cubes
2 10-3/4 oz. cans cream of
  mushroom soup
2 4-oz. cans mushrooms,
  drained

2 c. red wine or beef broth
1-1/2 oz. pkg. onion soup mix
3 to 4 c. prepared egg noodles

Combine all ingredients except noodles in a 2-quart casserole dish. Cover and bake at 350 degrees for 3 hours, stirring occasionally. Serve over prepared noodles. Serves 6 to 8.

Fabric glue is perfect for securing white snowflake buttons to stocking cuffs or table runners.

Wild Rice & Mushrooms

Nettie Paul
Paynesville, MN

*A flavorful casserole that's really simple to prepare. Don't let
the amount of liquid surprise you...it comes out perfectly!*

2/3 c. wild rice, uncooked
1/2 c. long-cooking rice,
  uncooked
1/4 c. green pepper, chopped
2 T. dehydrated mixed
  vegetables

1/4 c. butter, diced
2-1/2 oz. pkg. slivered almonds
3 14-1/2 oz. cans chicken broth
2 T. chicken-flavored soup base
8-oz. can mushroom stems and
  pieces

Combine all ingredients in a large bowl, stirring well to blend. Spoon
into a greased roasting pan. Bake, covered, for 30 minutes at
350 degrees. Reduce heat to 325 degrees and continue baking for
one additional hour. Makes 8 servings.

A glittered chipboard initial tops off any little gift box
in a snap...simply tie it to the box with ribbon.

Mom's Best Casserole

Teena Hippensteel
Fort Wayne, IN

My mom used to make this quick & easy casserole when we were growing up. It's been a family favorite for years.

1 c. elbow macaroni, uncooked
10-3/4 oz. can cream of
   mushroom soup
1 c. shredded Cheddar or Colby
   Jack cheese

2-1/2 oz. pkg. sliced dried beef,
   chopped
2 eggs, hard-boiled, peeled and
   chopped

Combine all ingredients in a large bowl. Spoon into a lightly greased 2-quart casserole dish. Bake, covered, at 375 degrees for 45 to 50 minutes. Let stand 5 to 10 minutes before serving. Serves 6.

Make circle shapes with a large paper punch, then apply them on a foam cone using découpage medium... a terrific snow-day craft for family & friends.

146

Ellie's Layered Reuben Bake

Ellie Brandel
Milwaukie, OR

For all those Reuben lovers in the world, here is a recipe just for you! The no-boil lasagna noodles are thinner than traditional lasagna noodles, so they don't need to be boiled before using. They really make this a fast-prep meal!

27-oz. can sauerkraut, drained
  and rinsed
1 lb. sliced deli corned beef,
  coarsely chopped
10-3/4 oz. can cream of
  mushroom soup
8-oz. bottle Thousand Island
  salad dressing
1-1/4 c. milk
1 onion, chopped
1 t. dry mustard
9 no-boil lasagna noodles
1 c. shredded Swiss cheese
1/2 c. plain dry bread crumbs
1 T. butter, melted

In a medium bowl, combine sauerkraut with corned beef; mix well. In another medium bowl, combine soup, salad dressing, milk, onion and mustard; mix well. Spread 1/2 cup soup mixture in the bottom of a 13"x9" baking pan that has been sprayed with non-stick vegetable spray. Place 3 lasagna noodles over soup mixture. Top with half the sauerkraut mixture, half the remaining soup mixture and 3 noodles. Continue layering with remaining sauerkraut mixture and 3 lasagna noodles; cover with remaining soup mixture. Sprinkle top of casserole with cheese and bread crumbs; drizzle with butter. Cover with aluminum foil and bake at 350 degrees for 45 to 50 minutes, until bubbly. Uncover and bake for 5 to 10 minutes longer, until golden. Allow to stand for 5 to 10 minutes before serving. Serves 6 to 8.

As much fun as when you were
a kid...buy new jammies
for everyone spending
Christmas Eve at your home!

Texas-Style Enchiladas

Lorri Vaughan
Hondo, TX

Try these layered enchiladas...quick & easy!

10-oz. can enchilada sauce
12 6-inch corn tortillas, divided
12-oz. pkg. shredded Cheddar
   cheese, divided
1 lb. ground beef
1 T. chili powder

1 T. ground cumin
1/2 c. salsa
4-oz. can diced green chiles
Optional: 1/2 c. water
1 onion, finely chopped

Pour sauce into an ungreased 16"x12" baking pan. Arrange 6 tortillas across bottom of pan. Set aside 1-1/2 cups cheese. Spoon equal amounts of remaining cheese in center of each tortilla. Arrange remaining tortillas on top and set aside. In a medium skillet, brown ground beef with chili powder and cumin; drain. Add salsa and chiles to skillet; mix well and cook until heated through. If a thinner sauce is desired, add water and simmer 5 minutes. Spread meat sauce evenly over enchiladas. Top enchiladas with remaining cheese and onion. Bake, uncovered, at 350 degrees for 15 minutes. Allow to stand 5 minutes before serving. Makes 6 servings.

Simple touches say "welcome" when family & friends visit...
a snowman doormat, Christmas dishes and music
playing cheerily in the background will get
everyone in the holiday spirit.

Cozy Casseroles to Share

Taco Lasagna

Carol Hickman
Kingsport, TN

*Freeze one, eat one...what a time saver during the holidays.
When you're ready to bake the frozen lasagna, just thaw it
in the refrigerator for 8 hours, then bake as directed.*

2 lbs. ground beef chuck
2 1-1/4 oz. pkgs. taco
  seasoning mix
2 15-oz. containers ricotta
  cheese
4 egg whites, beaten
24 lasagna noodles, cooked

2 16-oz. pkgs. finely shredded
  Colby Jack cheese
2 24-oz. jars salsa
Garnish: Sour cream, sliced
  black olives, chopped
  green onions

Brown ground beef in a large skillet; drain. Stir in taco seasoning mix,
adding a small amount of water if a thinner sauce is desired. Remove
from heat and set aside. In a medium bowl, combine ricotta cheese
and egg whites until well blended. Lightly spray two, 13"x9" baking
pans with non-stick vegetable spray. In each baking pan, layer
4 lasagna noodles, 3/4 cup ricotta cheese mixture, half of ground beef
mixture and 1-1/3 cups shredded cheese. Next, layer each casserole
with 4 lasagna noodles, 3/4 cup ricotta cheese mixture, remaining
beef mixture, 1-1/2 cups salsa and 1-1/3 cups shredded cheese. Cover
one casserole with plastic wrap and freeze for up to 3 months. Bake
remaining casserole, uncovered, at 350 degrees for about 40 minutes,
or until hot and bubbly. Let stand for 10 minutes; garnish as desired
and serve. Makes 2 casseroles, each casserole makes 8 servings.

A pillar candle surrounded by a
ring of candy canes will add
a cheerful look to any room.
Keep the candy canes in place
with a rubber band hidden
by a ribbon tied in a bow.

Creamy Penne Pasta with Ham

Sherry Gordon
Arlington Heights, IL

Growing up in Peoria, this was one recipe Mom always made in the winter months. Cheesy and filling, it was perfect after a frosty day spent building snowmen or sledding.

8-oz. pkg. penne pasta,
   uncooked
10-3/4 oz. can cream of celery
   soup
1-1/4 c. milk
1-1/2 c. shredded mozzarella
   cheese, divided

2 c. French fried onions, divided
1 c. cooked ham, diced
1/3 c. tomatoes, chopped
1/2 c. frozen peas, thawed

Cook pasta according to package directions; set aside 3 cups cooked pasta. Reserve remaining cup for another recipe. In a medium bowl, stir together soup and milk until well blended. Stir in pasta, one cup cheese, one cup onions, ham, tomatoes and peas. Transfer to a greased 9"x9" baking pan. Bake, uncovered, at 375 degrees for 30 minutes, or until hot and bubbly; stir. Top with remaining cheese and onions. Bake for an additional 5 to 10 minutes, or until cheese melts and onions are golden. Serves 4.

Playful pompom garlands add frosty charm to mini trees...perfect for kids' rooms or as a table topper.

Cozy Casseroles to Share

Best-Ever Green Bean Bake

Connie Fortune
Bradford, OH

A sure potluck pleaser! Truly...just serve and watch it disappear.

10-3/4 oz. cream of
   mushroom soup
1/2 c. milk
1/8 t. white pepper

4 c. green beans, cooked
1-1/2 c. cooked ham, diced
1/2 c. Cheddar French fried
   onions

Mix together soup, milk, pepper, green beans and ham in a large bowl; spoon into a lightly greased 1-1/2 quart casserole dish. Bake, uncovered at 350 degrees for 25 minutes, or until hot and bubbly. Top with onions and bake 5 minutes longer. Makes 6 to 8 servings.

Paint tag-sale chairs white to turn them into extra seating
for family & friends. For a holiday look, thread
red & white ribbon through a mini wreath
and tie onto the back of each chair.

Marvelous Two-Dish Dinner

Becky O'Bryan
Meriden, CT

When the holidays are here, a make once, serve twice dinner is such a timesaver! Enjoy Meatloaf one night, and Shepherd's Pie the next.

Meatloaf:

2 lbs. lean ground beef
1 T. soy sauce
1/4 t. salt
1/8 t. pepper

1 egg, beaten
1/4 c. dry bread crumbs
12-oz. jar brown gravy, divided

Mix all ingredients except gravy together in a medium bowl. Spoon into a lightly greased 2-quart casserole dish. Add half the gravy; refrigerate remaining gravy for second meal. Bake meatloaf at 350 degrees for 20 minutes. Serve half of meatloaf; reserve half for second recipe. Makes 4 servings.

Shepherd's Pie:

Crumble reserved meatloaf into a lightly greased 2-quart casserole dish. Top with reserved gravy, layer on a drained 15-ounce can of corn; spread one cup mashed potatoes to cover all. Sprinkle with shredded Cheddar cheese to taste, about one cup. Bake, uncovered, at 350 degrees for 20 minutes. Makes 4 servings.

Small brown paper sacks chock-full
of wrapped candies are thoughtful
giveaways to hand out as sweet
"glad-you-stopped-by" gifts.

Stuffed Pepper Casserole

Jonel Neely
Gainesville, FL

*I love this recipe...all the flavor of stuffed peppers,
but in a quick-fix casserole.*

1 lb. ground beef
1 red pepper, diced
1 green pepper, diced
1 zucchini, diced
1 onion, diced
1 clove garlic, minced
1/2 t. cinnamon
1/2 t. ground cumin
salt and pepper to taste

1 T. cider vinegar
1 T. sugar
26-oz. jar pasta sauce
1 c. shredded Cheddar cheese
1 c. shredded mozzarella cheese
8-oz. pkg. medium egg noodles,
   cooked
Garnish: fresh parsley

Brown beef in a large skillet over medium-high heat. Add peppers,
zucchini and onion and cook until tender. Stir in garlic, cinnamon,
cumin, salt and pepper; cook one minute longer. Remove from heat. In
a bowl, stir together vinegar and sugar; mix in pasta sauce. Add to beef
mixture; stir in noodles. Place in a lightly greased 13"x9" baking pan;
top with cheeses. Bake, uncovered, at 375 degrees for 20 minutes,
or until heated through. Garnish with parsley before serving.
Makes 6 servings.

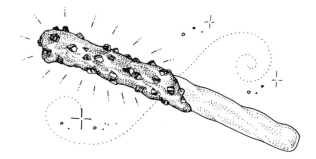

Dip bread sticks in melted dark chocolate, then roll in
crushed nuts for a sweet after-dinner treat.

153

Potluck Potato Bake

Trisha Donley
Pinedale, WY

I love to bring these potatoes to potlucks...
I always come home with an empty pan!

32-oz. pkg. frozen diced
   potatoes, thawed
16-oz. container sour cream
1 onion, chopped
8-oz. pkg. shredded Cheddar
   cheese

10-3/4 oz. can cream of
   celery soup
3/4 c. butter, melted and divided
2 c. corn flake cereal, crushed

In a large bowl, stir together potatoes, sour cream, onion, cheese, soup and 1/4 cup butter. Pour into a greased 13"x9" baking pan. In a medium bowl, toss cereal and remaining butter together; spread over top of casserole. Bake, covered, at 350 degrees for one hour and 15 minutes. Uncover and bake for an additional 15 minutes. Makes 16 to 20 servings.

Make gift wrapping sweet & simple...tuck cookbooks
into tea towels and tie with kitchen string.

Sausage & Veggie Bake

Tina Begley
Russell Springs, KY

To keep from crying when chopping onions, keep them in the refrigerator. When you chop a cold onion, you'll never cry again!

1 to 2 T. oil
1 c. celery, chopped
1/2 c. green pepper, chopped
1/2 c. onion, chopped
2 c. water
2.1-oz. chicken noodle soup mix

3/4 c. instant rice, uncooked
1 lb. ground pork sausage,
  cooked, drained and
  crumbled
Optional: 4-oz. can sliced
  mushrooms, drained

Heat oil in a small skillet over medium heat. Cook celery, green pepper and onion for 5 minutes; set aside. Bring water to boil in a medium saucepan. Add soup mix, cover and simmer for 5 minutes. Stir in rice and remove from heat. Cover; let stand 5 minutes. In a greased 13"x9" baking pan, mix together sausage and rice mixture. Stir in vegetable mixture and mushrooms, if using. Bake, uncovered at 350 degrees for 20 minutes, or until heated through. Makes 6 to 8 servings.

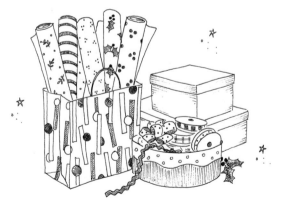

Cover a table with giftwrap...kids big & little will love it!

Easy Chicken Divan

Lori Ritchey
Denver, PA

This is an easy yet elegant dish for company or
church suppers...just serve with rice or noodles.

10-3/4 oz. can cream of
    chicken soup
1/2 c. mayonnaise
1/2 t. lemon juice
1/2 t. curry powder
4 to 6 boneless, skinless
    chicken breasts, cooked

10-oz. pkg. frozen broccoli
    spears, thawed
1/4 c. bread crumbs
1/2 c. butter, melted
8-oz. pkg. shredded Cheddar
    cheese

In a medium bowl, blend together soup, mayonnaise, lemon juice and
curry. Arrange chicken and broccoli in a greased 13"x9" baking pan;
cover with soup mixture. Toss bread crumbs with melted butter;
spoon over top of casserole. Sprinkle with cheese. Bake, covered,
at 350 degrees for 20 minutes. Uncover and bake for an additional
10 minutes. Makes 4 to 6 servings.

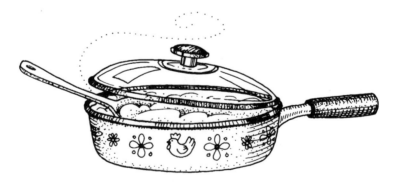

Garlicky orzo is a tasty side for any main dish. Sauté 2 cloves
chopped garlic in 2 tablespoons butter until garlic is golden.
Remove from heat and stir in one tablespoon lemon juice,
one cup cooked orzo and 2 tablespoons chopped parsley.

Ruby's Catalina Chicken

Ruby Dorosh
Shippensburg, PA

*A winning combination...savory chicken baked
with a tangy dressing and sweet jam.*

2 t. oil
6 boneless, skinless chicken
   breasts

1/2 c. Catalina salad dressing
1/2 c. apricot jam
3 T. onion soup mix

Heat oil in a large skillet over medium-high heat. Add chicken; cook 4 minutes on each side, or until golden and juices run clear. Remove chicken to a lightly greased 3-quart casserole dish. Stir together dressing, jam and soup mix in small bowl; pour over chicken. Bake, covered, at 350 degrees for 45 minutes, or until chicken is cooked through. Makes 6 servings.

Fill a watering can with garden tools, seed
packets and a gift card to a favorite nursery...
a gardening friend will be so tickled!

Chop Suey Casserole

Beverly Tierney
Elida, OH

Growing up, I spent a lot of time with my dear aunt who lived in the country. On cold winter nights she would prepare this casserole. Even today, it brings back warm memories of those times.

1 lb. ground beef
2 onions, chopped
1 c. celery, chopped
1/4 c. soy sauce
10-3/4 oz. can cream of
  mushroom soup
10-3/4 oz. can cream of
  chicken soup
1-1/2 c. warm water
1/2 c. long-cooking rice,
  uncooked
3-oz. can chow mein noodles

Brown ground beef in a large skillet over medium heat; drain. Stir in onions, celery, soy sauce, soups, water and rice. Transfer to a lightly greased 13"x9" baking pan. Bake, covered, at 350 degrees for 45 minutes. Sprinkle chow mein noodles over top. Return to oven, uncovered, for 15 minutes. Makes 6 servings.

Stuff stockings with gift cards, woolly socks, cocoa packets, teabags, soup mixes, CD's or DVD's...then just listen for the squeals of delight Christmas morning!

Fast-Fix Chicken & Rice

Karen Lehmann
New Braunfels, TX

*Bakes in just 20 minutes...a must-have
when family & friends are visiting.*

8-oz. pkg. chicken-flavored
   vermicelli rice mix, cooked
4 boneless, skinless chicken
   breasts, cooked and cubed
10-3/4 oz. can cream of
   mushroom soup

1/2 c. sour cream
1 c. shredded Cheddar cheese
1/2 c. bread crumbs

In a large bowl, combine cooked rice mix, chicken, soup and sour cream. Spoon into a greased 11"x7" baking pan. Top with cheese, then layer on bread crumbs. Cover and bake at 350 for 20 minutes, or until cheese is melted and bubbly. Makes 4 servings.

Pick up a package of refrigerated mashed potatoes
at the grocery for a quick & easy side dish. Heat,
and stir in cream cheese, sour cream and butter
to taste...as yummy as homemade.

Farmhouse Squash Bake

Loyce Wright
Pampa, TX

Although I had never tried this recipe before, I made and delivered this casserole to share with friends. Later, I received a letter letting me know how wonderful this casserole was, and they all wanted the recipe. So, of course, I had to make it again, to see what all the fuss was about. They were right, it is very good.

3 lbs. yellow squash, sliced
1 onion, chopped
1/4 c. butter
2 T. all-purpose flour

12-oz. can evaporated milk
1/2 lb. American cheese, diced
1 c. potato chips, crushed

Combine squash and onion in a stockpot of salted water. Simmer over medium-low heat until tender, 5 to 10 minutes. Drain and place in a greased 2-quart casserole dish; set aside. In a saucepan over medium heat, melt butter. Whisk in flour, a little at a time; add milk gradually. Stir in cheese and simmer over low heat until cheese melts. Pour sauce over squash mixture; sprinkle top with potato chips. Bake, uncovered at 350 for 30 minutes. Serves 8 to 10.

A whimsical snowman with apple eyes, a pine cone nose, greenery for eyebrows and a mustache (u-shaped bobby pins hold greenery in place), is sure to give your neighbors a smile!

Cheesy Chicken & Vegetables

Michelle Fredrick
Laura, OH

Every time I make this recipe, it reminds me of my teenage years at Sheila's home. Sheila's mother often made this for us. It's so quick & easy to prepare, and has such a wonderful taste, that now I make it for my family. They absolutely love it.

2 10-3/4 oz. cans cream of
   mushroom soup
10-3/4 oz. can cream of
   chicken soup
10-3/4 oz. can cream of
   celery soup
1/2 c. milk
3 15-oz. cans mixed vegetables,
   drained

2 9-3/4 oz. cans chicken,
   drained
6 c. cooked rice
16-oz. pkg. shredded Cheddar
   cheese
16-oz. pkg. shredded
   mozzarella cheese

In a large saucepan over low heat, blend soups and milk over low heat. When soup mixture is warm, stir in vegetables and chicken. Cook for another one to 2 minutes. Remove from heat and set aside. Spoon rice into a lightly greased 13"x9" baking pan; pour soup mixture over rice. Top casserole with shredded cheeses. Bake, uncovered, at 350 degrees for 25 to 30 minutes, or until casserole is bubbly and cheese is lightly golden. Serves 8 to 10.

While the family is gathered together, pile everyone in the car for a trip around town to see the Christmas lights and decorations...sweet memories in the making.

Chicken & Sausage Supreme

Sharon Brown
Orange Park, FL

So tasty, and with only 4 ingredients, you'd better double this recipe!

4 to 6 chicken breasts, cooked
    and chopped
1 lb. ground pork sausage,
    browned and drained

5-oz. pkg. yellow rice, cooked
10-3/4 oz. can cream of
    chicken soup

In a large bowl, combine chicken and sausage. Add rice and stir well; blend in soup. Spoon into a lightly greased 11"x7" baking pan. Bake, uncovered, at 350 degrees for 20 to 30 minutes, or until golden and heated through. Serves 4 to 6.

Glue peppermint sticks or candies to the edges of picture frames, let dry and slip pictures inside.

Cozy Casseroles to Share

Rancho Grande Casserole

Monica Cantrell
Taylor, AZ

This recipe is from my aunt...it's great for feeding a crowd!

1-1/2 lbs. lean ground beef
2 onions, chopped
1 green pepper, chopped
3 8-oz. cans tomato sauce
2 16-oz. can kidney beans,
   drained and rinsed
2 c. cooked rice

2 t. chili powder
1-1/2 t. salt
2 15-oz. cans tamales
1 c. shredded Cheddar cheese
Garnish: 2-1/4 oz. can sliced
   black olives, drained

In a large skillet, lightly brown beef with onions and green pepper; drain. Stir in tomato sauce, kidney beans, rice, chili powder and salt. Spoon into a lightly greased 13"x9" baking pan. Bake, covered, at 350 degrees for 40 minutes. Remove from oven and arrange tamales on top of casserole. Spoon chili sauce from tamales over top; sprinkle with cheese. Return to oven and continue baking, uncovered, 20 minutes longer. Garnish with sliced olives. Makes 12 servings.

Use a snowflake or holly leaf-shaped cookie cutter to turn tortillas into tasty chips for dipping. Heat 1/2 inch of oil in a deep skillet over medium-high heat. Add cut-outs and cook for one minute, or until crisp, turning occasionally.

Savory Chicken & Stuffing

Lori Hurley
McCordsville, IN

If you'd like, this makes a terrific make-ahead meal. Simply cover after topping with cheese, and then refrigerate. When ready to bake, just follow the remainder of the recipe instructions.

7 slices white bread, crusts
   trimmed
4 c. cooked chicken, chopped
8-oz. can sliced mushrooms,
   drained
8-oz. can sliced water chestnuts,
   drained
10-3/4 oz. can cream of
   mushroom soup

10-3/4 oz. can cream of
   celery soup
1/2 c. mayonnaise
4 eggs, beaten
2 c. milk
1 t. salt
1 c. shredded Cheddar cheese
2 c. herb-flavored stuffing mix
1 c. butter, melted

Cut each bread slice into 4 triangles. Arrange in a lightly greased 13"x9" baking pan. Layer chicken, mushrooms and water chestnuts over bread. Combine soups and mayonnaise in a medium bowl; spread over top. In a medium bowl, mix together eggs, milk and salt; pour over casserole. Sprinkle top with cheese. In a medium saucepan, sauté stuffing in melted butter. Spread over top of casserole. Bake, covered, at 350 degrees for one hour. Uncover and bake an additional 15 minutes. Makes 6 to 8 servings.

A time-saving dessert...layer apple pie filling with creamy whipped topping in parfait glasses. Top off servings with a sprinkle of cinnamon...yum!

Taco Casserole

Jill Valentine
Jackson, Tennessee

*This casserole bakes in 30 minutes, making it ideal
for a quick-fix dinner during the holidays.*

2 lbs. ground beef
1-1/4 oz. pkg. taco
   seasoning mix
1/4 c. water
1 c. sour cream
8-oz. pkg. shredded Mexican-
   blend cheese

8-oz. tube refrigerated crescent
   rolls
2 c. nacho-flavored tortilla
   chips, crushed
Garnish: shredded lettuce,
   salsa, sour cream,
   chopped tomatoes

In a skillet over medium heat, brown beef; drain. Add taco seasoning and water; mix well. Stir in sour cream. Press crescent rolls into a lightly greased 13"x9" baking pan. Spread ground beef mixture evenly over rolls; sprinkle with cheese. Top with tortilla chips. Bake, uncovered, at 350 degrees for 25 to 30 minutes, until crescent rolls are golden. Garnish as desired. Serves 8 to 10.

Bake up oodles of gingerbread men...hanging from the tree,
marching across a mantel, or piled in a bowl, they
add a little cheer to holiday decorating.

Overnight Faux Lasagna

Juanita Lint
Forest Grove, OR

This recipe came from a 1980 North Dakota church recipe book.
It is a big hit...as tasty as lasagna, but without the effort.
That's how the name came about!

16-oz. pkg. wide egg noodles
1 T. butter, melted
8-oz. pkg. cream cheese,
  softened
1 c. cottage cheese with chives

1/2 c. sour cream
1 lb. ground beef
1/3 c. dried, minced onion
8-oz. can tomato sauce
salt and pepper to taste

Cook half the package of noodles in boiling water for 5 to 6 minutes; drain and reserve remaining uncooked noodles for another recipe. Arrange half the cooked noodles in a greased 2-quart casserole dish. Spread noodles evenly with melted butter. In a medium bowl, combine cream cheese, cottage cheese and sour cream. Spoon mixture over noodles. Arrange remaining cooked noodles over cream cheese mixture; set aside. In a skillet, brown ground beef and onions; drain well. Combine beef mixture with tomato sauce, salt and pepper to taste; spoon over noodles. Cover and refrigerate for one to 8 hours. Uncover and bake at 350 degrees for 30 minutes. Cover with aluminum foil and bake for an additional 15 minutes. Makes 10 to 12 servings.

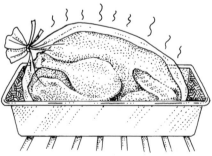

Keep some oven roasting bags on hand for baking holiday ham, chicken or turkey. The bags will speed up the cooking time, plus there's no roaster to clean up...just toss the bag!

estive

Family Desserts

New England Cranberry Pie

JoAnn
Gooseberry Patch

A friend who lives on Deer Isle, Maine whipped up this yummy dessert for our family. It's absolutely delicious!

1 c. whipping cream
1/4 c. sugar
1/2 t. vanilla extract
8-oz. pkg. cream cheese,
   softened

16-oz. can whole-berry
   cranberry sauce
9-inch shortbread cookie crust

In a chilled bowl, using an electric mixer with chilled beaters, beat cream, sugar and vanilla on medium speed. Continue to beat until soft peaks form. Set aside. In a large bowl, beat cream cheese until fluffy; gradually add cream mixture, beating until smooth. Reserve a few whole cranberries from cranberry sauce. Fold remaining cranberry sauce into cream cheese mixture. Spoon mixture into pie crust. Freeze for 4 hours, or until firm. Remove pie from freezer and let stand at room temperature for 15 minutes before serving. Garnish individual slices with reserved whole cranberries. Serves 8.

Family fun...build a yummy gingerbread house and top it off with chocolate bar doors and shutters!

Mom's Bread Pudding

Cheri Emery
Quincy, IL

I always remember this recipe of my mother's. She served it with the cinnamon sauce, and I really think that's what made it different from other bread pudding recipes. Mom didn't actually have a recipe for this, so I had to stand in the kitchen with her one day watching her every move, so we could figure out the exact measurements. I think we figured it out perfectly...another wonderful memory of Mom in her beloved kitchen.

3 eggs, beaten	1 t. cinnamon
3 c. milk	1 t. nutmeg
3/4 c. sugar	8 slices white bread, cubed
1 t. vanilla extract	

Whisk together eggs and milk in a large bowl; stir in sugar, vanilla, cinnamon and nutmeg. Arrange bread cubes in a buttered 3-quart casserole dish. Pour egg mixture over bread, gently pressing cubes down so they will soak up all the egg mixture. Set aside for 30 minutes. Bake at 350 degrees until firm, about 40 minutes. Spoon warm Cinnamon Sauce over servings. Serves 8.

Cinnamon Sauce:

1/2 c. sugar	1 c. cold water
1/2 t. cinnamon	1/4 c. margarine, sliced
1 T. cornstarch	1 t. vanilla extract

In a small pan, combine sugar, cinnamon and cornstarch. Stir in water and margarine. Cook over medium heat until mixture thickens. Stir in vanilla.

Little nibbles...use mini cookie cutters to cut out stars, bells and snowflakes from slices of sweet quick breads.

Snowball Cake

Joyce Loszewski
Windham, NH

This recipe was handed down to me from my mom, who got it from the owner of a dairy farm where my mom worked as their bookkeeper. It's light and not very sweet, and is a favorite of my son, Rob, at Christmastime.

1 T. unflavored gelatin
1/4 c. cold water
1 c. boiling water
1 c. sugar
1/8 t. salt
1 c. orange juice

juice of 1 lemon
1 pt. whipping cream, divided
1 angel food cake, torn
Optional: 3-1/2 oz. can
sweetened flaked coconut

In a large bowl, soften gelatin in cold water. Stir in boiling water to dissolve gelatin. Add sugar and salt; stir well. Blend in orange and lemon juices; mix well. Chill mixture until firm. Spray a 4-quart round bowl with non-stick vegetable spray; set aside. With an electric mixer on medium speed, whip one cup cream until soft peaks form; fold into gelatin mixture. In the sprayed bowl, layer 1/3 gelatin mixture and half of cake pieces. Repeat layering, ending with gelatin mixture on top. Refrigerate overnight. Turn chilled cake out onto a serving platter. Whip remaining cream until stiff peaks form, adding sugar to taste. Frost the top of the cake with whipped cream; sprinkle with coconut, if desired. Serves 10.

Hot glue together 4-inch long cinnamon sticks to make fragrant coasters for mugs of tea or cocoa.

Cheri's Red Velvet Cake

*Cheri Crocker
Anderson, SC*

This very moist cake is great for Christmas!

18-1/4 oz. pkg. red velvet
   cake mix
18-1/4 oz. pkg. milk chocolate
   cake mix

2 c. walnuts, crushed

In separate bowls, prepare cake batters according to package directions. Combine both batters in a large bowl; mix well. Pour into 2, greased and floured 13"x9" baking pans. Bake at 350 degrees for 30 to 40 minutes, until a toothpick inserted near the center comes out clean. Let cakes cool for one hour; turn out of pans onto serving plates. Prepare Fluffy Icing and spread over sides and tops of cakes; sprinkle with walnuts. Makes 2 cakes, each serving 10 to 12.

Fluffy Frosting:

2 8-oz. pkgs. cream cheese,
   softened
2 16-oz. pkgs. powdered sugar

1 c. margarine, softened
2 t. vanilla extract
milk

In a large bowl, combine cream cheese and powdered sugar. Beat with an electric mixer set on medium speed. Add margarine and vanilla; blend well. Add milk, a teaspoon at a time, until desired consistency is achieved.

Place a tasty pie or cake in
a basket and deliver to a
busy friend...she'll love it.

Struffoli

Pam Littel
Pleasant View, TN

Struffoli has been made by our family for generations. Every year, between Christmas and New Year's, my children and I spend a day rolling, cutting and frying. The time we spend cooking and talking is priceless.

2 c. all-purpose flour	oil for frying
1/4 t. salt	1 c. honey
3 eggs	1 T. sugar
1 t. vanilla extract	Optional: sprinkles

In a large bowl, whisk together flour and salt. Add eggs, one at time, mixing well by hand. Stir in vanilla. Turn dough out onto a lightly floured surface and knead, 5 minutes, until smooth. Divide dough in half and roll out each half to form a 1/4-inch thick rectangle. Cut rectangle into 1/4-inch wide strips and roll each strip into a pencil shape, about 7 inches long. Slice each pencil-shaped roll into 1/4 to 1/2-inch pieces. Add enough oil to a deep skillet to equal 2 inches. Over medium-high heat, fry several pieces of dough at a time until golden. Drain on paper towels; place in a large bowl. Repeat with remaining dough. In a small skillet over low heat, cook honey and sugar together for 5 minutes. Remove from heat and drizzle over fried pieces; stir gently to coat. Remove from bowl with a slotted spoon; arrange on a large platter. Decorate with sprinkles, if desired. Refrigerate until ready to serve. Serves 12.

Begin a Christmas scrapbook and fill it with copies of letters to Santa, wish lists and holiday photos... what fun to read year-after-year.

Dianna's Best Tiramisu

Dianna Oakland
Titusville, FL

I have tried many versions of this dessert, this one is by far the best.
Everyone always asks for seconds...and the recipe!

1 c. coffee, brewed and cooled
1/2 c. plus 1 T. sugar, divided
2 8-oz. pkgs. cream cheese, softened
2 T. almond-flavored liqueur or 1/4 to 1/2 t. almond extract

12-oz. container frozen whipped topping, thawed
16-oz. pound cake, sliced into 30 slices
1 T. baking cocoa

In a medium bowl, combine coffee and one tablespoon sugar; set aside. Using an electric mixer set on medium speed, beat cream cheese until fluffy; add remaining sugar and almond liqueur or extract. Gently fold in whipped topping and set aside. Layer 10 cake slices on the bottom of a ungreased 13"x9" baking pan. With a pastry brush, apply 1/3 of coffee mixture to cake. Top with 1/3 of cream cheese mixture. Repeat 2 more times to create 3 layers. Sprinkle cocoa over top and refrigerate overnight. Makes 16 to 24 servings.

Dip the rim of a mug into melted chocolate, then quickly
dip the rim in crushed peppermints. Fill with creamy
cocoa and marshmallows, then sit back and enjoy.

Homemade Gingerbread Cake

Dee Ann Ice
Delaware, OH

This is a wonderful recipe that will make your entire home smell delicious when you bake it. Don't skip the sauce... it's what takes this recipe over the top!

2 c. all-purpose flour
1 t. baking powder
1 t. baking soda
1/2 t. salt
2 t. ground ginger
1 t. cinnamon
1 t. nutmeg

1/4 t. ground cloves
1/2 c. shortening
1/2 c. sugar
1 c. molasses
1 c. buttermilk
1 egg, beaten
Garnish: whipped topping

In a large bowl, combine first 8 ingredients; set aside. In a separate large bowl, blend together shortening and sugar with an electric mixer set on medium speed. Beat in molasses. Add dry mixture and buttermilk alternately to molasses mixture, beating well after each addition. Stir in egg. Spoon batter into a greased and floured 13"x9" baking pan. Bake at 350 degrees for 40 to 45 minutes, or until a toothpick comes out clean. To serve, cut cake into squares; top with Warm Vanilla Sauce and a dollop of whipped topping. Serves 12 to 15.

Warm Vanilla Sauce:

1 c. brown sugar, packed
2 T. all-purpose flour
1 c. water

1 T. butter
1/2 t. vanilla extract
1/8 t. salt

In a saucepan, mix sugar and flour together. Add remaining ingredients; cook and stir over medium heat until thickened.

Slip a packet of spiced cider, cocoa or herbal tea
into a Christmas card for a special friend...
she'll be absolutely delighted.

Gotta-Have-It Holiday Cake

Thomas Golden
Waverly, NY

A holiday hasn't passed in my life without this cake being the crowning topper to every meal. It originated with my grandmother, and my mother now has passed the recipe down to my children. Once the smell of coffee starts wafting through the air, it's time for this must-have dessert!

16-oz. pkg. angel food cake mix
1 pt. whipping cream
1 T. vanilla extract

5-oz. chocolate candy bar, chopped

Prepare and bake cake mix according to package directions. Using an electric mixer set on medium speed, whip cream until soft peaks form; add vanilla. Melt chocolate bar in a double boiler over hot water; fold into whipping cream mixture. Place cake on a cake stand; frost top and sides of cake with whipped cream mixture. Chill for one to 2 hours. Makes 12 to 16 servings.

They went through the Raisin and Almond Gate, into a wonderful little wood where gold and silver fruit hung from the branches, tinsel sparkled and there was a scent of oranges all around. This was Christmas Wood.
-E.T.A. Hoffman, The Nutcracker

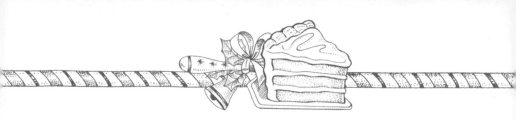

Date Torte

Lucille Nelimark
Manistique, MI

It's the sprinkling of chocolate chips that makes this torte special.

1 c. chopped dates
1 t. baking soda
1 c. boiling water
2 T. butter or margarine
1 c. sugar
1 egg, beaten

1/2 t. vanilla extract
1/8 t. salt
1-1/2 c. all-purpose flour
12-oz. semi-sweet chocolate
   chips

Toss together dates and baking soda in a medium bowl. Pour boiling water over mixture; set aside to cool. In a separate bowl, blend together butter or margarine and sugar. Beat in egg; add vanilla and salt. Pour into cooled date mixture; stir in flour. Mixture will be very thin. Pour into a greased 13"x9" baking pan. Sprinkle batter with chocolate chips. Bake at 350 degrees for 40 minutes; let cool. Cut into squares to serve. Makes 20 servings.

Turn store-bought whipped cream into something really special....stir in 2 to 3 tablespoons of a favorite-flavor jam, then dollop over slices of pie or cake.

Mattie Lou's Prune Cake

Betty Sanders
Townville, SC

This recipe was handed down from my grandmother, Mattie Lou, who would only make it during the Christmas holiday. It has been a tradition each Christmas and is a special request at Thanksgiving by my son, Brian, and husband, Keith.

2 c. sugar
2 c. self-rising flour
1 T. cake spice
3 eggs, beaten
1 c. oil

4 2-1/2 oz. jars prune
   baby food
1 t. vanilla extract
Optional: 3/4 c. chopped pecans

Mix sugar, flour and cake spice together in a large bowl. Blend in eggs, oil, prunes and vanilla; mix thoroughly. Stir in pecans, if desired. Pour batter into a greased and floured tube pan. Bake at 350 degrees for approximately one hour, until a toothpick inserted in center comes out clean. Let cool on wire rack. Makes 12 to 14 servings.

Making some surprise balls to unwrap on Christmas Eve helps everyone settle in before the big morning. Wrap crepe paper 'round -and-'round little toys and candies until the paper forms a ball. Everyone will love unwinding the paper until the surprise is found inside!

Ultimate Peanut Butter Pie

Irene Putman
Canal Fulton, OH

This recipe has been in our family for a very long time. I got it from my husband's grandmother many years ago. At first glance it resembles pecan pie, but, surprise...it's the best peanut butter pie you've eaten. Everyone wants the recipe and you'll be a very popular cook when you bake this easy-to-make pie.

1 c. light corn syrup	1/3 c. crunchy peanut butter
1/2 t. vanilla extract	9-inch pie crust
1 c. sugar	Optional: whipped cream
3 eggs, beaten	

Blend together all ingredients except pie crust and whipped cream in a medium bowl. Pour into pie crust and bake at 400 degrees for 15 minutes. Reduce heat to 350 degrees and continue to bake an additional 30 to 35 minutes. Filling should be set slightly more around the edges than in the center. Serve plain or with whipped cream, if desired. Serves 6 to 8.

Slice 'n Bake
Sugar Cookie Dough

Beginning in early December, mix up batches of cookie dough and pop in the freezer. Jot down the baking directions on a mailing tag and tie to the freezer bag. Later in December, when it's time to bake cookies, just remove from the freezer and bake.

Mom's Snow Pie

Shelly Richards
Plain City, OH

My 94 year-old grandma and I share January birthdays, and this recipe is one my mom would make to celebrate our birthdays. Mom had a passion for baking and trying new recipes, and this was an immediate hit!

3 egg whites, beaten
1 t. vanilla extract
3/4 c. sugar
1 t. baking powder
1 c. round buttery crackers,
    crushed

1/2 c. chopped pecans
4 1-oz. sqs. sweet baking
    chocolate, grated and divided
Garnish: whipped topping

With an electric mixer on medium speed, beat egg whites and vanilla until soft peaks form; set aside. Combine sugar and baking powder in a separate bowl. Gradually add to egg whites; beat until stiff peaks form. Fold in cracker crumbs, pecans and chocolate, reserving 2 tablespoons chocolate for garnish. Spread mixture into a greased 9" pie plate. Bake at 350 degrees for 25 minutes. Cool completely. Top with whipped cream and reserved chocolate. Refrigerate until ready to serve. Makes 6 to 8 servings.

Sweet treats are sure to be a welcome surprise nestled inside a vintage picnic tin. Tie a ribbon on the handle and slip in a sprig of greenery...so thoughtful.

Pistachio Puff

Lisa Spell
New Port Richey, FL

I have very fond memories of this recipe because it was my mom's favorite Christmas dessert. Simply put...it's tasty and delicious.

8-oz. container frozen whipped topping
3.4-oz. pkg. instant pistachio pudding mix
1 c. chopped walnuts
1 c. sweetened flaked coconut

15-1/4 oz. can crushed pineapple, drained
10-oz. jar maraschino cherries, drained
3 c. mini marshmallows

In a medium bowl, combine whipped topping and pudding mix; blend well. In a separate bowl, combine nuts, coconut, pineapple, cherries and marshmallows; blend into pudding mixture. Chill for 30 minutes before serving. Makes 10 servings.

Here's an easy way to make new ornaments look vintage. Set them in a glass bowl on a windowsill for a few months....the sunlight will soften their colors.

Coconut Freezer Cake

Tracie Spencer
Rogers, KY

*This recipe has always been around, but recently I rediscovered it and
it has become a favorite of mine. Everyone always comments how
much better this recipe is than traditional coconut cakes.*

18-1/4 oz. pkg. white cake mix
14-oz. pkg. sweetened flaked
  coconut
16-oz. container sour cream

2 c. sugar
8-oz. container frozen whipped
  topping, thawed

Prepare cake according to package directions dividing batter evenly
among three, 9" round cake pans. Bake according to package
directions. Let cool. In a large bowl, combine coconut, sour cream and
sugar; set aside one cup of mixture. Place one cake on a cake stand
and top with half the coconut mixture. Add second cake and spread
remaining coconut mixture on top. Place third layer on; set aside.
Combine reserved coconut mixture with whipped topping; frost top
and sides of cake. Place in freezer. Let stand 15 minutes before
serving. Makes 12 to 18 servings.

Fill an apothecary jar with old-fashioned ribbon candy...
pretty to look at and sweet to enjoy!

Karey's Mocha Cake

Karey Leroy
Folsom, CA

I was given this recipe by a friend in 1984 and have been making it ever since. It turns out best in cool weather, so I usually make it for Thanksgiving and Christmas dinners.

18-1/4 oz. pkg. devil's food
   cake mix
4 eggs, beaten
1 c. sour cream
1 c. coffee-flavored liqueur

3/4 c. oil
6-oz. pkg. semi-sweet chocolate
   chips
Garnish: chocolate frosting or
   powdered sugar

In a large bowl, combine first 5 ingredients. Beat with an electric mixer on low speed for 2 minutes. Increase speed to medium-high and beat 5 additional minutes. Stir in chocolate chips; pour batter into a greased and floured Bundt® pan. Bake at 350 degrees for 50 to 55 minutes. Let cake cool in pan for 30 minutes. Turn cake out onto a cake stand to cool completely. Before serving, drizzle with melted chocolate frosting or dust with powdered sugar. Makes 20 to 24 servings.

It's simple to give votive holders a frosty look. Coated with spray adhesive, then rolled in mica snow, candles tucked inside will glimmer.

Cocoa & Coffee Sheet Cake

Patricia Ivey
Lamar, AR

My family really enjoys this scrumptious cake!

2 c. all-purpose flour
2 c. sugar
1/2 c. shortening
1/4 c. baking cocoa
1 c. brewed coffee
1/2 c. butter

1 t. baking soda
1 t. vanilla extract
1/2 c. buttermilk
1 t. cinnamon
2 eggs, beaten

In a large bowl, combine flour and sugar; set aside. In a saucepan, combine shortening, cocoa, coffee and butter; bring to a boil. Slowly stir into flour mixture. Batter will resemble fudge. Stir in baking soda, vanilla, buttermilk, cinnamon and eggs, mixing until well blended. Pour batter into a greased and floured 13"x9" baking pan. Bake at 400 degrees for 25 minutes. Pour frosting over cake immediately after removing cake from oven. Makes 24 servings.

Frosting:

1/4 c. baking cocoa
6 T. milk
1/2 c. butter

16-oz. pkg. powdered sugar
1 t. vanilla extract
1/2 c. chopped pecans

In a saucepan, combine cocoa, milk and butter; bring to a boil. Add powdered sugar, vanilla and pecans, stirring well.

Drizzle melted chocolate over cakes or cookies the easy way...dip the tines of a fork into the chocolate, then do the drizzling.

Date Pudding

Christine Zimmerman
Berne, IN

I can remember my grandmother would make Date Pudding for just about every holiday or family get-together. As a child I would never try it, but when I got older, I discovered it was really good and so simple to make!

1 c. sugar	2 T. butter, melted
1 c. chopped dates	1 c. milk
1 c. bread crumbs	Optional: 1-1/2 c. mini
1 t. baking powder	marshmallows
1 egg, beaten	

Mix together sugar, dates, bread crumbs and baking powder in a large bowl. Stir in egg, butter and milk, blending well. Pour mixture into a lightly greased 1-1/2 quart casserole dish. Bake at 325 degrees for one hour, or until top looks dry. If desired, add marshmallows over top of pudding and return to oven for 5 minutes, or until melted. Serves 6.

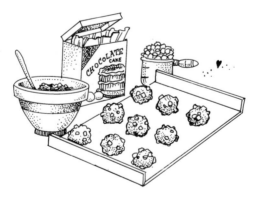

Whip up cake-mix cookies when it's time for a classroom party or holiday bazaar. Blend together a 9-ounce package of devil's food cake mix with one beaten egg, one tablespoon melted shortening, 2 tablespoons water and 1/2 cup chopped nuts. Drop by teaspoonfuls onto a greased baking sheet and bake at 350 degrees for 10 minutes. Makes 2 dozen.

Mini Mincemeat Sweets

Marlene Darnell
Newport Beach, CA

Tiny bites of yummy mincemeat topped with a drizzling of sweet frosting...perfect!

1 c. butter, softened	2 c. all-purpose flour
8-oz. pkg. cream cheese, softened	1/4 t. allspice
	1-1/3 c. mincemeat pie filling
3/4 c. powdered sugar	1/4 c. milk

With an electric mixer on medium speed, beat together butter and cream cheese. Add powdered sugar and beat until fluffy. Beat in flour and allspice until well blended. Chill dough for one hour, or until easy to handle. On a lightly floured surface, roll out 1/3 of dough to 1/8-inch thick; keep remaining dough chilled until ready to roll out. Cut out dough with a 2-1/2 inch round cookie cutter. Place circles on ungreased baking sheets. Spoon one teaspoon mincemeat onto half of each circle of dough. Fold over other half; seal edges well with a fork. Brush milk over dough. Bake at 350 degrees for 15 minutes, or until lightly golden. Cool on a wire rack. Drizzle frosting over cooled pastries. Makes 5 dozen.

Frosting:

1 c. powdered sugar	1/4 t. vanilla extract
	2 T. milk, divided

In a small bowl, stir together powdered sugar, vanilla and one tablespoon milk. Stir in additional milk, one teaspoon at a time, until frosting reaches a drizzling consistency.

An adorable garland...use
mini clothespins to show off a
collection of holiday handkerchiefs.

Eggnog Pound Cake

Nancy Cohrs
Donna, TX

*This is a cake that reminds me of sweet Christmases
and favorite family gatherings.*

1 c. butter, softened
1 c. shortening
3 c. sugar
6 eggs, beaten
3 c. all-purpose flour

1 c. eggnog
1 t. lemon extract
1 t. vanilla extract
1 t. coconut extract
1 c. sweetened flaked coconut

Blend together butter and shortening using an electric mixer on
medium speed. Gradually add sugar; beat until fluffy. Add eggs, one
at a time, beating well after each addition. Use a spoon to stir in flour
alternately with eggnog. Blend in extracts and coconut. Pour into
a greased and floured 10" tube pan. Bake at 325 degrees for
1-1/2 hours; cool for 10 minutes before removing from pan. Makes
12 to 14 servings.

A pair of hinged shutters make a great spot for
keeping track of holiday wish lists, get-togethers,
church bazaar and classroom party dates...
simply tack up notes with poster putty.

Snowballs

Hope Davenport
Portland, TX

Here in South Texas we have to make these around the holidays because they are the only snowballs we are going to see. No snowball fights with these!

1 c. semi-sweet chocolate chips
1/3 c. evaporated milk
1 c. powdered sugar

1/2 c. chopped walnuts
1-1/4 c. sweetened flaked coconut

Combine chocolate chips and milk in a double boiler; heat over hot water until chocolate melts. Stir to blend well. Remove from heat; stir in powdered sugar and nuts. Cool slightly. Form into one-inch balls; roll in coconut. Makes about 2 dozen.

Keep a mix of of trimmings on hand for wrapping yummy treats to share...vintage-style buttons, holiday seals, mailing tags and ribbon all make take-home packages extra special.

Strawberry-Almond Trifle

Angie Venable
Delaware, OH

*I took this yummy trifle to a church Christmas social...
it was gone in a flash!*

1-1/4 c. cold milk
1-oz. pkg. instant sugar-free
  vanilla pudding mix
1/4 c. orange juice, divided
1/8 t. nutmeg
8-oz. container frozen whipped
  topping, thawed

1 pound cake
3 c. strawberries, hulled and
  halved and divided
1/4 c. sliced almonds, toasted
  and divided

Pour milk into a large bowl. Add dry pudding mix, 2 tablespoons orange juice and nutmeg; whisk together for one minute. Gently fold in whipped topping; set aside. Slice cake horizontally into 4 layers. Sprinkle layers evenly with remaining orange juice; cut into one-inch cubes. Place half the cake cubes in a trifle bowl or large clear glass bowl. Top cubes with 2-1/2 cups strawberries and 2 tablespoons almonds. Spoon half the whipped topping mixture over berries and almonds. Layer remaining cake cubes and whipped topping. Garnish with reserved berries and almonds. Refrigerate until ready to serve. Makes 10 servings.

Chocolate-dipped peppermint sticks are tasty take-home gifts for visiting friends. Arranged in a cello bag tied with red rick rack, these sweets will be a reminder of time spent together.

Sweet Cherry Flan

Mary Murray
Mt. Vernon, OH

*I first tasted flan at a friend's home many years ago. When I prepare
this easy slow-cooker version, I dollop servings with homemade
whipped topping and lightly dust with cinnamon.*

5 eggs, beaten
1/2 c. sugar
1/2 t. salt
3/4 c. all-purpose flour
12-oz. can evaporated milk

1 t. vanilla extract
16-oz. pkg. frozen dark sweet
   cherries, thawed and drained
Garnish: whipped cream

Beat eggs, sugar and salt with an electric mixer on high speed until
mixture is thick and yellow. Add flour; beat until smooth. Add
evaporated milk and vanilla; beat well. Pour batter into a well-greased
slow cooker. Arrange cherries evenly over batter. Cover and cook on
low setting for 3-1/2 to 4 hours, or until flan is firm. Garnish
individual servings with whipped cream. Serves 6.

Fill pint-size Mason jars with red cinnamon candies
and nestle a votive in the center. They'll look so
welcoming lighting the walkway to your door.

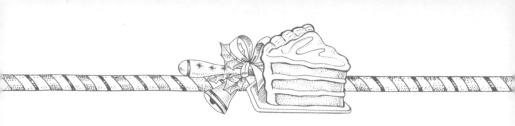

No-Bake Fruitcake

Jenny Prince
Huntington, WV

This recipe is all-time family favorite...it's so delicious!

16-oz. pkg. marshmallows
3/4 c. evaporated milk
6 c. graham cracker crumbs
16-oz. pkg. walnuts

16-oz. pkg. pecans
16-oz. pkg. candied fruit,
   chopped
16-oz. pkg. raisins

Combine marshmallows and milk in a double boiler; heat over hot water until marshmallows melt. Stir to blend and remove from heat. Add crumbs, nuts, candied fruit and raisins; stir well to blend. Line a 6"x3-3/4" or 8"x4" loaf pan with plastic wrap. Spoon fruit mixture into pan. Cover with aluminum foil and refrigerate overnight. To serve, invert pan, remove plastic wrap and slice. Makes 60 pieces.

Create a gift-wrapping station where supplies are easy to find. Fill pails and baskets with bows and wrap, tuck scissors and trims inside Mason jars...a place for everything!

Raisin Spice Cake

Barbara Ferree
New Freedom, PA

This is a recipe that my mother made at Christmastime. Looking back, we don't understand why we had it just during the holidays, as it is a delicious cake to be enjoyed throughout the whole year! Mother always served it with a homemade chocolate icing, but it's just as delicious sprinkled with powdered sugar.

16-oz. pkg. raisins
2 c. brown sugar, packed
2 eggs, beaten
1/4 c. shortening
1/4 c. margarine, softened

1 c. buttermilk, divided
1 t. baking soda
2 c. all-purpose flour
1 t. cinnamon
1/2 t. ground cloves

Place raisins in a medium saucepan; add water to cover. Simmer over medium heat for 5 minutes. Drain and set aside. Blend brown sugar, eggs, shortening and margarine together in a large bowl. Add 1/2 cup buttermilk; stir well and set aside. Dissolve baking soda in remaining buttermilk. Thoroughly combine flour, brown sugar mixture, baking soda mixture, cinnamon and cloves. Add raisins and stir. Pour batter into 2 greased and floured 9" round baking pans. Bake at 350 degrees for 35 to 40 minutes, or until center tests done. Makes 16 to 18 servings.

A magnetic knife holder is a handy spot to keep track
of holiday lists. Attach lists with magnetic buttons
from the craft store that have been spruced up
with hot-glued-on buttons.

Mince Ice Cream Pie

Jacque Thompson
Clarkston, WA

A new taste for mincemeat pie lovers...this is cool and creamy!

1-1/2 qts. French vanilla ice
   cream, softened
1-1/2 c. mincemeat pie filling,
1/2 c. plus 2 T. chopped walnuts
   or pecans, divided

9-inch graham cracker crust
Optional: sweetened whipped
   cream

In a large bowl, combine ice cream, mincemeat and 1/2 cup chopped nuts; mix well. Spread in graham cracker crust; freeze until firm, 2 to 3 hours. Before serving, spoon whipped cream over pie, if desired. Garnish with remaining nuts. Serves 8 to 10.

To make fragrant, no-bake cinnamon-applesauce ornaments blend together one cup cinnamon, 3/4 cup applesauce and 1/4 cup white glue. Roll out the dough and cut with cookie cutters...remember to use a drinking straw to make a small hole at the top of the ornaments if you'd like to hang them.

Charlotte's Cocoa Cake

Carol Levy
San Jose, CA

This recipe was the first cake my mother-in-law, Charlotte Levy, ever served when I first met her back in 1977. She loved baking and was generous in sharing many recipes with me. The pure cocoa really gives us chocolate addicts what we crave!

2 c. sugar
1 c. butter, softened and divided
2 eggs, beaten
1/2 c. buttermilk
2 t. vanilla extract, divided
1/2 c. baking cocoa, divided
1 c. boiling water

2 c. all-purpose flour
1 t. salt
1 t. baking soda
1 t. cinnamon
1/2 c. milk
2 c. powdered sugar
Optional: 1 c. chopped pecans

In a large bowl, with an electric mixer on medium speed, blend together sugar and 3/4 cup butter. Add eggs, buttermilk and one teaspoon vanilla; beat until well blended. In a small bowl, whisk 1/4 cup cocoa into boiling water. Add to sugar mixture and blend well. In a medium bowl, combine flour, salt, baking soda and cinnamon. Add to cocoa mixture and beat with an electric mixer on low speed to combine thoroughly. Pour batter into a greased and floured 13"x9" baking pan. Bake at 350 degrees for 25 to 30 minutes, or until a toothpick inserted in center comes out clean. In a small saucepan over high heat, whisk together remaining cocoa and milk; bring to a boil. Remove from heat; add remaining butter. Stir until butter has melted. Whisk in powdered sugar and remaining vanilla; mix until smooth. Stir in pecans, if using. Pour mixture over warm cake. Serve warm or at room temperature. Serves 12.

Cardboard egg cartons are a terrific way to store ornaments safely until next Christmas.

Friendship Peppermint Mud Pie

Lori Vincent
Alpine, UT

Each year for Christmas, I get together with four dear friends for Christmas brunch. For the past 12 years, we've met once a month at a different home to craft together. It's a great time for us to have "girl time" and share what's going on in our lives. At Christmas, we traditionally eat pie, so whenever I make this recipe, I always think of my best friends!

14-oz. pkg. chocolate sandwich cookies, crushed and divided
6 T. butter
1/2 gal. peppermint ice cream

16-oz. jar hot fudge ice cream topping
8-oz. container frozen whipped topping, thawed

Set aside 1/4 cup cookie crumbs. Combine remaining cookie crumbs and melted butter in a large bowl. Toss to coat. Transfer to a greased 13"x9" baking pan; press firmly to cover bottom of pan. Slice ice cream into 1/2-inch slices and layer over crumb crust. Freeze until solid. At serving time, spoon fudge topping over ice cream and spread whipped topping to edges. Garnish with reserved cookie crumbs. Makes 12 servings.

Craft a yo-yo wreath to share with girlfriends...you can make bunches in no time at all. Simply glue fabric yo-yos to a ring form and let dry.

Cookies & Cocoa Get-Together

Grandma Elda's Jam-Jam Cookies

Wendy Parente
Brunswick, OH

This recipe was handed down from my Great-Grandma Elda. I remember helping my mom mix all the ingredients in one of her well-worn mixing bowls in the kitchen on our small Ohio farm. I was so impatient waiting for the dough in the freezer to set up! I think my favorite part of making these cookies was the jam she would let my sister and me spread between the cookie sandwiches.

1 c. butter, softened
1 c. brown sugar, packed
1/4 c. milk
1/2 t. vinegar
1 t. vanilla extract
2 c. all-purpose flour

1 t. baking soda
1/2 t. salt
2 c. quick-cooking oats, uncooked
12-oz. jar red raspberry or 12-oz. jar blackberry jam

In a large bowl, blend butter and brown sugar together with an electric mixer set on medium speed. In a small bowl, combine milk, vinegar and vanilla; add to butter mixture. Blend well. Beat in flour, baking soda and salt. Reduce mixer speed to low; add oats a little at a time until mixture resembles pie dough. Shape dough into a 2-inch diameter log. Wrap dough with wax paper and freeze for at least 2 hours. Cut dough in 1/4-inch slices; place on an ungreased baking sheet. Bake at 350 degrees for 10 minutes. Place cookies on wire racks to cool. Spread one teaspoon of desired flavor jam on half the cookies. Top with remaining cookies to make sandwiches. Makes 3-1/2 to 4 dozen.

Animal crackers and cocoa to drink,
that is the finest of suppers I think.
When I am grown and can have what
I please, I think I shall always
insist upon these.
-Christopher Morley

Candy Bar Cookies

Lori Graham
Pittsfield, PA

For many years when my children were young, my very special friend along with her children and I would make Christmas cookies together. This recipe was one of her wonderful family traditions that she shared with my family. The cookies always took a little time to make, but they tasted like Christmas.

2 c. plus 2 T. butter, softened
   and divided
3 c. powdered sugar, divided
1/4 c. milk
3 t. vanilla extract, divided
1/2 t. salt
4 c. all-purpose flour

14-oz. pkg. caramels,
   unwrapped
1/2 c. plus 1/3 c. evaporated
   milk, divided
1 c. chopped nuts
6-oz. pkg. semi-sweet chocolate
   chips

In a large bowl, blend together 1-1/2 cups butter and 1-1/2 cups powdered sugar. Stir in milk, 2 teaspoons vanilla, salt and flour; blend well. Chill for 2 hours. On a lightly floured surface, roll dough to 1/4-inch thickness. Cut with a 2-1/2 inch round cookie cutter. Arrange on an ungreased baking sheet; bake at 325 degrees for 12 to 16 minutes. Let cool. Prepare caramel topping by combining caramels and 1/2 cup evaporated milk in the top of a double boiler; stir until caramels have thoroughly melted. Remove from heat; stir in 1/2 cup butter, one cup powdered sugar and chopped nuts. Top each cookie with one teaspoon caramel mixture; set aside. In a medium saucepan, combine chocolate chips and remaining evaporated milk over medium heat. Stir until chocolate chips have melted. Remove from heat and stir in remaining butter, vanilla and powdered sugar. Spread chocolate mixture on each cookie over caramel topping. Makes 3 dozen.

Friends & family will love receiving an invitation to a cookies & cocoa get-together... especially when invitations are tucked into woolly mittens or snow caps.

Christmas Peppermint & Chocolate Meringues

Peggy Cummings
Cibolo, TX

Use the ice pulse button on your blender
to make quick work of crushing the candies.

2 egg whites
1/8 t. cream of tartar
1/8 t. salt
3/4 c. sugar
1/2 t. vanilla extract

3 T. peppermint candies, crushed
2 c. mini semi-sweet chocolate chips

In a large bowl, beat egg whites with an electric mixer at high speed until foamy. Add cream of tartar and salt, beating until mixed. Gradually add sugar, one tablespoon at a time, beating well after each addition until stiff peaks form. Gently fold in remaining ingredients. Drop by teaspoonfuls 1-1/2 inches apart on baking sheets sprayed with non-stick vegetable spray. Bake at 250 degrees for 40 minutes, or until dry. Remove to wire racks to cool completely. Store in an airtight container. Makes 3 dozen.

Snow globes are a quick craft to make with friends. Use silicone glue to secure a plastic or ceramic figure to the inside of a jar lid; let dry. Fill the jar almost to the top with distilled water, a pinch of glitter and a dash of glycerin (to keep the glitter from falling too quickly.) Tighten the lid and let it snow!

Pizzelle

Joanna Nicoline-Haughey
Berwyn, PA

These are a traditional Italian cookie that I bake during the Christmas season. When I was growing up, my grandmother and mother always had a batch on hand.

6 eggs, beaten
1-1/4 c. sugar
1/2 c. oil
1 t. anise seed

1 T. vanilla extract
1/2 c. butter, melted
2 c. all-purpose flour

Beat all ingredients except flour together with an electric mixer on medium speed. Using a spoon, stir in flour and mix by hand until well blended. Drop by teaspoonfuls onto a hot pizzelle iron; bake about 20 to 25 seconds. Remove with a fork and stack to cool. Makes 5 dozen.

Date Crispies

Kim Faulkner
Delaware, OH

A yummy cookie swap treat!

3/4 c. plus 1-1/3 T. butter
1 c. sugar
8-oz. pkg. chopped dates
2 eggs, beaten

1 c. chopped pecans or walnuts
2 c. crispy rice cereal
1 c. sweetened flaked coconut

Melt butter in a large skillet over medium-low heat. Combine sugar and dates; add to skillet, stirring often. Cook until mixture starts to thicken. Stir in eggs, blending quickly to keep them from cooking. Stir until well blended. Increase heat to medium-high. Boil mixture, stirring constantly, for 1-1/2 to 2 minutes. Remove from heat. Blend in nuts and cereal. Cool until comfortable to handle. Form into one-inch balls; roll in coconut. Cool on wax paper. Makes 2 dozen.

Gingerbread Men

Kimberly Pfleiderer
Galion, OH

I love to make these sweet ginger cookies...they make the house smell great and they taste so good!

2-1/4 c. all-purpose flour
1/2 c. sugar
1 t. baking powder
1/2 t. baking soda
1/2 t. salt
1-1/2 t. cinnamon

1 t. ground ginger
1/4 t. ground cloves
1/2 c. shortening
1/2 c. molasses
1 egg, beaten
Optional: frosting, sprinkles

In a large bowl, whisk together flour, sugar, baking powder, baking soda, salt and spices. In a separate bowl, blend together shortening, molasses and egg; stir into flour mixture and blend well. Shape dough into a ball; wrap in wax paper and refrigerate for one hour, or until dough is firm. On a lightly floured surface, roll out dough to 1/8 to 1/4-inch thickness and cut with a cookie cutter. Arrange on an ungreased baking sheet. Bake at 350 degrees for 8 minutes, or until golden. Frost and decorate, if desired. Makes about 2 dozen.

Dress up simple shortbread cookies with a yummy cinnamon glaze. Combine ½ cup cinnamon baking chips with one teaspoon shortening in a microwave-safe bowl. Microwave on high for one minute, stir, then drizzle cookies with glaze.

Great-Grandma Musselman's Cookies

Joyce Keeling
Mansfield, MO

It wouldn't be Christmas without my Great-Grandma Musselman's ginger cookies. She always baked these cookies for Christmas and they always had to have pink frosting. They stay soft in a tightly covered container for weeks...if they last that long!

1 c. sugar	1 t. cinnamon
1 c. shortening	2 t. ground ginger
2 eggs, beaten	1 T. baking soda
1 c. molasses	2 T. hot water
5 c. all-purpose flour	1 T. vinegar

In a large bowl, blend together sugar and shortening. Beat in eggs, molasses, flour and spices. Dissolve baking soda in hot water; stir in vinegar and add to flour mixture. Divide dough into thirds and roll out on a lightly floured surface to about 1/8-inch thickness. Cut out with round cookie cutters and arrange on an ungreased baking sheet. Bake at 350 degrees for 10 minutes, or until very lightly golden around edges. Cool; frost with Fluffy Frosting. Makes about 6 dozen.

Fluffy Frosting:

1 egg white, beaten	1/2 c. light corn syrup
2 T. sugar	1/2 t. vanilla extract
1/8 t. salt	1 drop red food coloring

Combine all ingredients except vanilla and food coloring in a double-boiler over medium heat. Heat water in bottom of double-boiler over medium-high heat; do not bring water to a boil. Using an electric mixer, beat mixture 8 minutes, or until stiff peaks form. Remove from heat; stir in vanilla and food coloring to tint a soft pink. Beat until thick enough to spread.

Nellie's Persimmon Cookies

Dorothy Ames
Lerna, IL

These are very delicious! This recipe was my mom's and I have passed it down to my children. My mom would bake them at Christmas to share...now I do the same for my children and their families.

1 persimmon	2 eggs, beaten
1 c. margarine, softened	2-1/2 c. all-purpose flour
1 c. brown sugar, packed	1/2 t. baking soda
1 c. sugar	1 c. chopped pecans

Rinse persimmon under cold water; pat dry. Make an x-shaped cut in the pointed end with a small sharp knife. Pull back sections of the peel from cut end; discard seeds. Discard peel and stem end. Process in food processor or in a blender until smooth. Measure out 1/2 cup. Save remaining pulp for another recipe. Beat together margarine and sugars in a medium bowl. Blend in eggs and persimmon. In a separate bowl, combine flour and baking soda; add to margarine mixture. Fold in pecans; refrigerate dough for one hour. Drop dough by teaspoonfuls onto an ungreased baking sheet. Press each cookie down with a fork dipped in warm water. Bake at 350 degrees for 15 to 20 minutes, or until golden. Makes 4-1/2 dozen.

Make spirits bright by stitching pompoms
onto plain winter hats, scarves and mittens.
Super-easy to do with just a needle & thread!

Fruitcake Cookies

Jane Baumann
Waverly, OH

This rich cookie makes enough for sharing at a cookie swap!

1/2 c. shortening
1-1/2 c. brown sugar, packed
2 eggs, beaten
2 c. all-purpose flour
1/2 t. baking soda
1/2 t. salt
1 t. cinnamon

1/4 t. ground cloves
2 c. golden raisins
2 c. diced mixed candied fruit
Optional: 1-1/2 c. chopped nuts
1/2 c. evaporated milk
2 t. vinegar

Blend together shortening and brown sugar; beat in eggs. In a separate bowl, mix together flour, baking soda, salt and spices; mix well. Stir in raisins, fruit and nuts, if using. Add to shortening mixture along with milk and vinegar; mix well. Drop by teaspoonfuls onto greased baking sheets. Bake at 325 degrees for 20 to 25 minutes. Makes about 6 dozen.

It's easy to find dark, semi-sweet and milk chocolate cocoa mixes at the grocery, as well as white chocolate and raspberry-chocolate flavors. Set out a variety of mixes and everyone is sure to find one to enjoy... and maybe even a new favorite.

Chocolate-Cherry Bars

Sandy Taylor
Macomb, IL

This recipe is so good! If you're short on time, instead of frosting them, you can just dust them with powdered sugar.

18-1/4 oz. pkg. chocolate
   cake mix
21-oz. can cherry pie filling
1 t. almond extract
2 eggs, beaten

1 c. sugar
1/3 c. milk
5 T. margarine or butter
6-oz. pkg. semi-sweet chocolate
   chips

With an electric mixer on medium speed, beat together cake mix, pie filling, almond extract and eggs in a large bowl. Spread into a greased and floured 15"x10" jelly-roll pan. Bake at 350 degrees for 20 to 30 minutes, or until toothpick inserted near center comes out clean. Remove from oven and set aside. Combine sugar, milk, margarine or butter in a small saucepan. Bring to a boil over medium heat; boil for one minute. Remove from heat; stir in chocolate chips until melted and smooth. Pour and spread over warm bars; cool completely. Cut into bars. Makes about 1-1/2 dozen.

Cheery Cherry Punch

Beth Bundy
Long Prairie, MN

My grandma made this years ago...it was always a must at get-togethers.

3-oz. pkg. cherry gelatin mix
1 c. hot water
46-oz. can pineapple juice,
   chilled

4 c. apple juice, chilled
3/4 c. lemon juice
1 ltr. ginger ale, chilled

Stir gelatin mix and hot water in a small bowl until gelatin is dissolved. Pour into a large pitcher, stir in juices; chill. When ready to serve, add ginger ale to pitcher, gently stirring to combine. Makes 3 quarts.

Pam's Almond Bars

Pam Kittle
Clay City, IN

I sometimes add red or green food coloring to the dough at Christmastime. The recipe is easily doubled and they freeze well too.

1/2 c. butter, softened
2 eggs, beaten
1 t. almond extract

1 c. sugar
1 c. all-purpose flour
Garnish: powdered sugar

Whisk together all ingredients except powdered sugar; press into a greased 8"x8" baking pan. Bake at 350 degrees for 17 to 20 minutes. Cool slightly; slice into small squares. Gently roll in powdered sugar. Makes about 16.

Mexican Hot Chocolate

Barb Bargdill
Gooseberry Patch

This yummy hot chocolate is spiced up with a pinch of cinnamon.

1/2 c. water
1/3 c. honey
5 T. baking cocoa
1/2 t. cinnamon

1/8 t. nutmeg
1/4 t. salt
4 c. milk
1 t. vanilla extract

Combine first 6 ingredients in a large, heavy saucepan. Bring to a boil over medium-high heat, stirring constantly. Gradually add milk and vanilla extract, stirring constantly with a whisk. Heat to 180 degrees or until tiny bubbles form around edge, without boiling, stirring with a whisk. Makes 8 servings.

Homemade snow cones...pour orange, cranberry, pomegranate or pineapple juice over scoops of freshly fallen snow.

205

Laced Mocha Nut Pats

Brenda Melancon
Gonzales, LA

I needed something different when it came to cookie recipes for the holiday season this year, so I created this one. I love the combination of chocolate and nuts!

3/4 c. butter, softened
1/4 c. powdered sugar
2 T. baking cocoa
3 T. instant espresso coffee
   powder
3 T. coffee-flavored liqueur or
   3/4 t. chocolate extract

17-1/2 oz. pkg. chocolate chip
   cookie mix
1-1/2 c. pecans, ground
Garnish: powdered sugar

In a large bowl, combine butter, powdered sugar, cocoa, espresso powder and coffee liqueur or extract. With an electric mixer set on low speed, beat for 30 seconds. Increase speed to medium; beat until creamy. Gradually add cookie mix and pecans; beat until well blended. Roll dough into 1-1/4 inch balls. Place 2 inches apart on parchment paper-lined baking sheets. Bake at 350 degrees for 11 minutes. Let cool on baking sheets 2 minutes; remove to wire racks to cool completely. Dust with powdered sugar. Makes 6 dozen.

It's fun to play games on a wintry day when family & friends come to visit. Pull out all the best board and card games, along with puzzles and blocks. Set out lots of yummy snacks and turn up the Christmas music...terrific for all ages!

Chocolatey Cream Pies

Jennifer Chandler
Locust Grove, GA

I have always loved oatmeal cream pies and chocolate chip cookies. One day, while perusing the recipes in my collection, I thought, "Hey! Why not combine the two for the queen of all cookies!" And that's what I did. I must tell you, however, these cookies can become addictive. I've had friends unable to stop eating them!

1-1/4 c. butter, softened	1 t. baking soda
1 c. brown sugar, packed	1/2 t. salt
1/2 c. sugar	1/4 t. cinnamon
1 egg, beaten	3 c. quick-cooking oats,
1 t. vanilla extract	uncooked
1 t. rum or rum extract	12-oz. pkg. semi-sweet
1-1/2 c. all-purpose flour	chocolate chips

With an electric mixer on medium speed, beat butter and sugars until creamy. Add egg, vanilla and rum or rum extract, beating well. Whisk together flour, baking soda, salt and cinnamon in a large bowl. Stir in oats and chocolate chips. Add dry ingredients to wet ingredients and mix until well blended. Drop dough by rounded tablespoonfuls 2 inches apart on parchment paper-lined baking sheets. Bake at 375 degrees for 8 minutes. Set aside to cool. Spread one tablespoon Creme Filling over the bottom of half the cookies; top with remaining cookies. Makes 1-1/2 dozen.

Creme Filling:

1/2 c. butter, softened	1/2 t. vanilla extract
2 c. powdered sugar	1/2 t. rum or rum extract
1 to 2 T. whipping cream	

With an electric mixer on medium speed, combine all ingredients until well blended. Increase mixer speed to high; beat until filling becomes light and fluffy.

Mexican Tea Cookies

Kimberly Pfleiderer
Galion, OH

It just wouldn't be Christmas without these cookies.

1 c. butter, softened
1/4 c. powdered sugar
2 t. vanilla extract
1 T. water

2 c. all-purpose flour
1 c. chopped pecans
Garnish: powdered sugar

With an electric mixer on medium speed, blend together butter and powdered sugar; add vanilla, water and flour. Stir in pecans. Shape dough in walnut-size balls. Arrange on an ungreased baking sheet. Bake at 300 degrees for 20 minutes. Remove from oven. While cookies are still hot, roll in additional powdered sugar. When cool, roll again in powdered sugar. Makes 3 dozen.

Peanut Butter Hot Chocolate

April Jacobs
Loveland, CO

So scrumptious...a must for peanut butter lovers!

1 c. milk
1 T. chocolate syrup

1 T. creamy peanut butter
Garnish: whipped cream

Heat milk in a saucepan over medium-low heat until heated through. Add chocolate syrup and mix well. Stir in peanut butter and stir until melted. Top with whipped cream. Makes one serving.

Take the family to a pottery painting class...what a fun time they'll have creating holiday plates and cups to share!

Grandma's Pecan Balls

Beckie Butcher
Elgin, IL

This is an old-fashioned favorite of mine. My Grandma Caroline always made these for Christmas...they were a treat I always looked forward to. They remind me of a truly old-fashioned holiday.

1 c. butter, softened
5 T. sugar
2 t. vanilla extract

2 c. all-purpose flour
2 c. pecans, broken
Garnish: powdered sugar

In a medium bowl, blend together butter and sugar; stir in vanilla and flour. Fold in pecans. Roll dough into walnut-size balls and arrange on an ungreased baking sheet. Bake at 300 degrees for 45 minutes. While still warm, sprinkle cookies with powdered sugar; sprinkle again before serving. Makes about 2 dozen.

Frosty-Fizzy Punch

Jacqueline Kurtz
Reading, PA

A scrumptious creamy combination of orange and vanilla...yum!

3 6-oz. cans frozen orange juice
   concentrate
2-1/4 c. water

3 T. vanilla extract
4 c. ginger ale, chilled
1 qt. vanilla ice cream

In a punch bowl, blend together orange juice concentrate, water, vanilla and ginger ale. Stir in ice cream to blend. Serves 10 to 12.

Chocolate-Pecan Drops

Meghan Hansen
Traverse City, MI

This recipe is the only must-have for our family at Christmas time. One taste of these brings back years of our family Christmas memories. My grandma made them for my mom as a little girl, then my mom made them for our family. Now, I am making them for our two little boys!

1 c. butter, softened	2 t. vanilla extract
2 c. sugar	4 c. all-purpose flour
8-oz. pkg. premelted	1 t. baking powder
unsweetened chocolate,	1 t. salt
divided	1 c. chopped pecans
2/3 c. milk	Garnish: red decorating sugar

With an electric mixer on medium speed, blend together butter and sugar. Add 4 pouches chocolate, reserving remaining pouches for another recipe, milk and vanilla; blend well. In a separate bowl, whisk together flour, baking powder and salt. Add to chocolate mixture; stir in nuts. Cover dough and chill 2 to 3 hours. Drop dough by rounded teaspoonfuls onto an ungreased baking sheet. Bake at 375 degrees for 7 minutes. Let cool on baking sheet 2 minutes; transfer to wire racks. Spread cookies with desired frosting and sprinkle with red sugar. Makes 3 dozen.

Frosting:

2 c. powdered sugar	red food coloring
2 T. hot water	1/2 t. peppermint extract
1 t. almond extract	green good coloring
1/2 t. anise extract	

Combine powdered sugar, hot water and almond extract in a medium bowl. Divide frosting between 2 bowls. To one bowl add anise extract and desired amount of red food coloring; stir well to blend. To the second bowl, stir in peppermint extract and desired amount of green food coloring; stir to blend thoroughly.

Cookies & Cocoa Get-Together

Amaretto Coffee

Katie Majeske
Denver, PA

*Several years ago I received a recipe from **Gooseberry Patch** for Christmas Morning Sticky Buns. That recipe, along with this one, has been our Christmas morning tradition for the last several years.*

1 c. whipping cream
1 T. sugar
1-1/2 t. almond extract

3/4 c. amaretto liqueur
12 c. hot brewed coffee
Garnish: chocolate shavings

With an electric mixer on medium speed, whip cream until it begins to thicken. Slowly add sugar and almond extract; continue beating until soft peaks form. To serve, add one tablespoon amaretto liqueur to each of 12 coffee cups. Fill with hot brewed coffee and top each with a dollop of whipped cream. Sprinkle with chocolate shavings and serve. Makes 12 servings.

Walnut Squares

Nancy Ramsey
Delaware, OH

Every year our family has a Sunday we set aside to bake cookies all day. This recipe was my dad's favorite. He has passed away, but we still bake them every Christmas remembering how much he loved them!

1/3 c. margarine
1 c. brown sugar, packed
1/4 t. salt
1 t. vanilla extract

1 egg, beaten
3/4 c. all-purpose flour
1 t. baking powder
1/2 c. chopped English walnuts

Combine all ingredients in a large bowl; mix well. Spread into a greased 9"x9" baking pan. Bake at 350 degrees for 30 to 40 minutes. Cut into small squares. Makes 16 to 20.

Make-Ahead Anise Cookies

Karen McCann
Marion, OH

My mother always baked these cookies each Christmas. And because they were always the first to disappear, she would hide them! These are also good with mint...just substitute peppermint oil.

3 eggs, room temperature
1 c. plus 2 T. sugar
1-3/4 c. all-purpose flour
1/2 t. baking powder
1/2 t. anise oil

With an electric mixer on medium speed, beat eggs until fluffy. Gradually add sugar and continue to beat for 20 minutes. Reduce speed to low; add flour and baking powder. Beat 3 minutes longer; add anise oil. Drop dough by tablespoonfuls onto a greased and floured baking sheet. Let stand overnight, uncovered. Bake at 325 degrees for 10 minutes. Makes 3 dozen.

Cinnamon Ice Cubes

April Garner
Independence, KY

This is a family favorite from Thanksgiving to New Year's Eve. Serve them in tall glasses of iced tea or soda.

1/2 c. red cinnamon candies
1/2 c. water
3 c. orange juice

Combine candies and water in a medium saucepan over medium heat. Bring to a boil; simmer, stirring constantly, until candies are dissolved. Add orange juice; mix well. Pour into ice cube trays; freeze. Makes 4 to 5 dozen.

Spiced Cranberry Tea

Patti McEachron
Burnsville, MN

A warm-you-to-your-toes sipper.

12-oz. pkg. cranberries
3 c. water
2-1/2 c. sugar
6-oz. can frozen orange juice
　concentrate
6-oz. can frozen lemonade
　concentrate

2 t. instant tea mix
10 drops cinnamon oil
12 drops clove oil
1 qt. apple juice, chilled

Boil cranberries in water until berries pop. Strain berries, reserving juice. To reserved juice, add remaining ingredients and bring to a boil. Remove from heat and cool. Keep syrup refrigerated. When ready to serve, add 1-1/2 cups water to one cup syrup and heat through. Makes 10 cups syrup or 40 servings.

Fill a milk bottle almost to the top with a yummy cocoa mix, then layer on mini marshmallows to fill the jar. Secure a square of wax paper over the top with kitchen string...a sweet gift for guests to take home with them.

Mom's Holiday Date Balls

Pamela Riley
Dedham, MA

When I was little, my three sisters and I would make homemade Christmas cookies with our mom. Although I loved all the different types we made, these tasty treats were among my favorite. They are so easy and delicious and bring back such sweet memories every time I bite into one.

1 c. butter
1 c. sugar
1/4 t. salt
8-oz. pkg. chopped dates

1-1/2 c. chopped pecans
2 c. crispy rice cereal
1 t. vanilla or rum extract
Garnish: powdered sugar

Melt butter in a medium saucepan over medium heat. Add sugar, salt and dates. Cook, stirring constantly, until mixture is smooth and thick. Remove from heat and stir in pecans, cereal and extract. Set mixture aside to cool. When cool, form into one-inch balls and roll in powdered sugar. Store in an airtight container. Makes 3 dozen.

Big and roomy, vintage bags are terrific tag-sale finds.
Use one for tucking lots of little gifts into...
a girlfriend will be delighted!

Nichole's Cake Mix Cookies

Nichole Martelli
Santa Fe, TX

*While baking Christmas cookies this year, I wanted to make a new cookie to add to the usual ones I give out. Not knowing what I wanted to do, I remembered that I had bought some cake mixes a few weeks earlier. After the first taste, my husband said, "Now that's a recipe that you have to send to **Gooseberry Patch**!" They are a flavorful and moist, but not-too-sweet cookie. This is definitely going to be a must-have on my Christmas cookie trays from now on.*

1/4 c. butter, softened
8-oz. pkg. cream cheese,
   softened
1 egg yolk, beaten

1/2 t. vanilla extract
18-1/4 oz. pkg. butter pecan
   cake mix

With an electric mixer on medium speed, blend together butter and cream cheese. Add egg yolk and vanilla; blend thoroughly. Gradually beat in dry cake mix. Dough will be slightly stiff. Cover and refrigerate dough for 20 minutes. Drop dough by rounded teaspoonfuls onto greased or parchment paper-lined baking sheets. Bake at 350 degrees for 14 minutes, or until lightly golden. Makes 3 dozen.

Top off a giftable garden book with a bouquet of beautiful hydrangeas you dried last summer...a sweet gift from the heart.

Eskimo Cookies

Gloria Robertston
Midland, TX

This was the first recipe I ever tried as a little girl. My mom helped me with it the first time, after that I could do it by myself. I have baked these cookies for many years...my children also used this recipe when they were learning to cook.

3/4 c. butter, softened
3/4 c. sugar
3 T. baking cocoa
1/2 t. vanilla extract

1 T. water
2 c. quick-cooking oats, uncooked
1 c. powdered sugar

Blend together butter and sugar in a large bowl. Add cocoa, vanilla and water; stir in oats. Refrigerate overnight covered. Form dough into 36 balls and roll in powdered sugar. Keep refrigerated until ready to serve. Makes 3 dozen.

Cocoa Bliss

Annette Ingram
Grand Rapids, MI

This will make you over-the-moon happy!

3 1-oz. sqs. milk chocolate
1 t. butter
1/4 t. vanilla extract

1 c. half-and-half
1 to 2 T. mini marshmallows
Garnish: nutmeg

Combine milk chocolate, butter and vanilla in a double boiler; stir until melted and smooth. Gradually add half-and-half; heat until hot without bringing to a boil. Serve over marshmallows; sprinkle with nutmeg. Makes one serving.

Christmas, children, is not a date.
It is a state of mind.
-Mary Ellen Chase

Hermit Cookies

Viveca Scott
Sacramento, CA

An old family recipe from my grandmother's family.
My mother made them every Christmas.

3/4 c. margarine, softened
2 c. brown sugar, packed
2 eggs, beaten
1 t. baking soda
1/2 c. boiling water

3 c. all-purpose flour
1 t. vanilla extract
1 c. raisins
Optional: 1 c. chopped nuts

Blend together margarine, brown sugar and eggs; set aside. Dissolve baking soda in boiling water; stir well to blend. Add flour to margarine mixture, alternating with soda mixture. Stir in vanilla, raisins and nuts, if using. Drop dough by heaping teaspoonfuls onto a greased baking sheet. Bake at 375 degrees for 10 to 12 minutes. Makes 2 dozen.

Best-Ever Hot Chocolate

Christy Bonner
Berry, AL

Every year when winter rolls around, I look forward to the cold nights we have here in Alabama just so I can make this hot chocolate. I usually just double the recipe and keep it warm in a slow cooker.

6 c. cold milk
3.9-oz. pkg. instant chocolate
   pudding mix

Garnish: whipped topping

Pour milk into a medium saucepan over medium heat. Add pudding mix and stir for one minute to blend. Bring just to a simmer; stir frequently. To serve, pour into mugs and top with whipped topping. Serves 6.

Cherry Pinwheels

Ruth Kletzien
Sheboygan Falls, WI

These are my husband's favorite Christmas cookie.
He says they taste like little cherry pies.

2 c. all-purpose flour
1 c. butter
8-oz. pkg. cream cheese

1/2 to 1 c. cherry preserves
2 egg whites, beaten
Garnish: sugar

Place flour in a large bowl. With a pastry blender or 2 forks, cut in butter and cheese until the mixture resembles large peas. Knead dough with hands until it cleans the bowl. Divide dough into quarters. Place one quarter of dough between 2 sheets of floured wax paper and roll out to an 8 or 9-inch square, 1/16-inch thick. Repeat with remaining dough. Wrap in wax paper and refrigerate overnight. When ready to bake, use a sharp knife to cut dough into 2-inch squares. Arrange squares on parchment paper-lined baking sheets. Using a sharp knife, make a one-inch diagonal cut from each corner to the center of each square. Place 1/2 teaspoon preserves in centers. Fold every other tip to the center over the jam to form a pinwheel. Lightly brush tops with egg white and sprinkle with sugar. Bake at 350 degrees for 12 to 15 minutes, until golden. Remove to cool on a wire rack. Makes about 5 dozen.

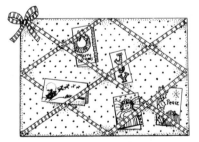

Keep holiday cards at hand with a sweetly beribboned board. Cover fiberboard with fabric, then stretch twill tape over the length of the board...staple loose ends to the back. Cards can then easily be slipped between the strips of ribbon.

Cranberry Cheesecake Bars

Patricia Wissler
Harrisburg, PA

*I have been making these bars for years. They look lovely
on a plate of Christmas cookies.*

2 c. all-purpose flour
1-1/2 c. quick-cooking oats,
  uncooked
3/4 c. plus 1 T. brown sugar,
  packed and divided
1 c. butter, softened
8-oz. pkg. cream cheese,
  softened

14-oz. can sweetened
  condensed milk
1/4 c. lemon juice
16-oz. can whole-berry
  cranberry sauce
2 T. cornstarch

In a large bowl, combine flour, oats, 3/4 cup brown sugar and butter, mixing until crumbly. Remove 1-1/2 cups of mixture and set aside for topping. Press remaining mixture into bottom of a 13"x9" baking pan lined with non-stick aluminum foil. Bake at 350 degrees until lightly golden, about 15 minutes. Set aside. In a medium bowl, beat cream cheese until smooth. Add condensed milk and lemon juice, whipping until completely combined. Pour evenly over warm crust. Spoon cranberry sauce into a bowl, stirring gently to blend. Add remaining brown sugar and cornstarch; mix to combine well. Drop cranberry mixture by tablespoonfuls over cream cheese layer. Sprinkle top with reserved crumb mixture. Bake at 350 degrees for 45 minutes, or until top is golden. Refrigerate until chilled. Cut into bars. Makes 3 dozen.

Fill a roomy basket with all the ingredients for a hot cocoa gift. Tuck in peppermint sticks, squares of chocolate, marshmallows and a favorite cocoa recipe. Add a few restaurantware mugs too...oh-so perfect for keeping chocolatey cocoa toasty warm!

INDEX

220

INDEX

INDEX

Send us your favorite recipe!

and the memory that makes it special for you!* If we select your recipe for a brand-new **Gooseberry Patch** cookbook, your name will appear right along with it...and you'll receive a FREE copy of the book.

Share your recipe on our website at
www.gooseberrypatch.com

Or mail to:
Gooseberry Patch • Attn: Cookbook Dept.
P.O. Box 812
Columbus, OH 43216-0812

* Don't forget to include your name, address, phone number and email address so we'll know how to reach you for your FREE book!

Find Gooseberry Patch
wherever you are!
www.gooseberrypatch.com

Call us toll-free at 1•800•854•6673

U.S. to Metric Recipe Equivalents

Volume Measurements

1/4 teaspoon	1 mL
1/2 teaspoon	2 mL
1 teaspoon	5 mL
1 tablespoon = 3 teaspoons	15 mL
2 tablespoons = 1 fluid ounce	30 mL
1/4 cup	60 mL
1/3 cup	75 mL
1/2 cup = 4 fluid ounces	125 mL
1 cup = 8 fluid ounces	250 mL
2 cups = 1 pint =16 fluid ounces	500 mL
4 cups = 1 quart	1 L

Weights

1 ounce	30 g
4 ounces	120 g
8 ounces	225 g
16 ounces = 1 pound	450 g

Oven Temperatures

300° F	150° C
325° F	160° C
350° F	180° C
375° F	190° C
400° F	200° C
450° F	230° C

Baking Pan Sizes

Square

8x8x2 inches	2 L = 20x20x5 cm
9x9x2 inches	2.5 L = 23x23x5 cm

Rectangular

13x9x2 inches	3.5 L = 33x23x5 cm

Loaf

9x5x3 inches	2 L = 23x13x7 cm

Round

8x1-1/2 inches	1.2 L = 20x4 cm
9x1-1/2 inches	1.5 L = 23x4 cm